amy butler's BLOSSOM

amy butler's
BLOSSOM

{ create *love* · express *beauty* · be *kind* }

ISSUES #1 & #2

CHRONICLE BOOKS
SAN FRANCISCO

First Chronicle Books LLC edition, published in 2015

Library of Congress Cataloging-in-Publication Data available.

ISBN 978-1-4521-4951-6

Manufactured in China

MIX
Paper from
responsible sources
FSC™ C016973

10 9 8 7 6 5 4 3 2 1

Chronicle books and gifts are available at special quantity discounts
to corporations, professional associations, literacy programs,
and other organizations. For details and discount information,
please contact our premiums department at
corporatesales@chroniclebooks.com or at 1-800-759-0190.

Chronicle Books LLC
680 Second Street
San Francisco, California 94107
www.chroniclebooks.com

CONTENTS

Welcome!

THIS IS BLOSSOM

I am Amy Butler. A designer of prints for fabrics, home, and fashion.

A few years ago I found myself at a crossroads in my business and life, and began seeking deeper meaning and happiness through amazing connections with other creatives, mentors, passionate dreamers, and spirited souls. I traveled the world to find new inspirations in cultures and traditions that I'd only read about in books.

That immersion has changed me. I realized my art was no longer just going to be making prints or designing things. It was going to be remaking me. Allowing all aspects of who I am to Blossom. I journaled my experiences and encounters both written and visually. My friends and family saw in my experiences a great experiment to share with the world. *Blossom* magazine was born.

These visual journals that have previously only been available as online magazines have been lovingly printed and assembled into what you are holding now. Issues #1 and #2 are contained here as a compendium of my expressions.

Books are for loving, and holding, and learning, and most of all, inspiration. I hope you enjoy *Blossom* as much as I love making it.

xo Amy

ISSUE # 1

amy butler's

Blossom

magazine

issue № 1 { create *love* express *beauty* be *kind* }

Be
beautiful
Be
yourself

CALLIGRAPHIES BY THICH NHAT HANH

BREATHE
IT ALL IN
LOVE IT
ALL OUT

welcome to
BLOSSOM!

I am so glad you're here!

I AM very excited to be writing this note of celebration! *Blossom* is the beginning of a beautiful story and I feel incredibly blessed to have the pleasure of creating this first issue. It's a juicy, gorgeous visual journal that's full of love and light! *Blossom* is truly the manifestation of positive change in my life that has transpired over the past two years. It's a pure expression of who I am and what I want to celebrate in the world. Cultivating *Blossom* allows me to connect with folks on all subjects that are close to my heart and provides me with a way to give to others. The curative quality and feel of this soulful art piece comes from my personal visions, hopes, and dreams. My main goal is to leave everyone who reads *Blossom* uplifted and inspired. I'm vibrating as I write this with a huge smile on my face . . . I love love love it and hope you will too!

"Beauty seen makes the one who sees it more beautiful."
~ *David Steindl-Rast*, A Listening Heart

Blossom is all about loving your life and living it beautifully with a spirited voice for creativity. You'll find experiences throughout the magazine that will help you tap into your heart and creativity through "how to" content, Blossom Club inspirational stories, quotes, and links to powerful life-changing resources. It's my dream to inspire folks to get in touch with the beauty in their lives and in themselves and to empower with love. The big story is about all of us expressing the vision in our hearts. I want us to understand that being connected to what we love is the greatest gift we can give the world and ourselves.

"The first recognition of beauty was one of the most significant events in the evolution of human consciousness. The feelings of joy and love are intrinsically connected to that recognition."
– *Eckhart Tolle from* A New Earth: Awakening to Your Life's Purpose

Blossom is about sharing and creating a community that inspires and supports each other. The essays and personal stories in the magazine are here to show us a reflection of our own brilliance. When we get to witness someone else's success, success meaning their pure connection to their joy, bliss, their real raw self, the wins, their challenges, their life's purpose; it's a big bright shiny mirror for us, and seeing that beautiful light and expression makes us think, "I recognize this, I have this same passion, and intense love inside me—yeah, this is possible, I can have a life I love, I can trust in connecting with my purpose and I have the courage to take the journey and unearth my magnificence. I have everything I need already inside of me." This inspiration is like a supercharged express ticket to developing the awareness of our gifts. The stories of inspiration are endless, and every one of us has one to share. Every human experience is a valuable experience and everyone has a gift to get out to the world and it's as simple as allowing it to happen, getting out of our own way and being ourselves. My life coach and dear friend Hildie Dunn says it so perfectly: "Magic is everywhere. In our community we remind each other that connecting to our gifts is not only possible, but for certain."

"A person's gift will make room for them, it will open doors because the nature of your gift will enlighten, motivate others, and snowball. You might not realize it's there, it's dormant, but others see it coming out. It's in your heart and it will radiate and lead us all to move on our destined path. It's a gift of love and a gift within."
~ *Calvin Miles*

Blossom is a reflection of all our journeys. The magazine itself was born out of our ability to grow through the challenges that have faced our business and personal life over the past two years. While looking towards our future, everything was turned a bit upside down, but in the messy transition we re-connected to our truth and the unlimited positive potential that change offers. Through Dave's inspiration to explore PDF patterns to complement our current patterns, I unearthed my deep passion to create a beautiful visual journal to uplift and send love into the world. Once we tapped into our truth and embraced the changes, universal support started flooding in! I'm still a bit scared and nervous, but I know in my heart we are where we are supposed to be and I'm willing to take the risks to keep this mojo going because it feels so good!

> "Life is a series of natural and spontaneous changes. Don't resist them - that only creates sorrow. Let reality be reality. Let things flow naturally forward in whatever way they like."
>
> ~ *Lao Tzu*

For Dave and I, the gifts of challenge have ignited clarity, positive change, and a true sense of purpose and joy. There's lots more digging to do. I know I'm just scraping the surface of what's in my heart. Will you join me on this journey? What are some of the challenges you've experienced that have transformed your life?

We honor each other by telling our truth and I am going to walk away from the "I'm only gonna show you my perfect stuff Amy," which has always been my safe go-to place for security and winning the acceptance of others. I've historically been a people pleaser, brilliant at building my outside world all the while the distractions kept me from fully connecting with my inner world and my feelings. I am on my path sorting this all out and seeing with every win and expansion that I am peeling away the layers of the onion, and that I want to continue practicing getting real and honest about how I want to feel in my life. I do see that a large part of my life has been true to my calling as I have been doing what I love for the past 20+ years, earning a lot of joy through taking risks and always only designing what I love, but it's different now, I'm seeing the new opportunities to power charge my life and that there's so much more I have to give. It's a great feeling to embrace the fact that we never stop expanding. For the first time in my life I'm loving who I am being in the world and loving myself and I want everyone to feel this way.

> "Let yourself be silently drawn by the strange pull of what you really love. It will not lead you astray."
>
> – *Jalaluddin Rumi*

We are meant to be happy, we are meant to love ourselves and love our lives. We have so much to give. We know we are in line with our gifts when we are happy, loving, and sharing, and it becomes more about who you are as a joyful, giving being rather than about what you do in a profession. In this place of alignment the universe supports us 100% no questions asked. We can risk, make new choices, be vulnerable, tell the truth about what we want most, and be in the moment, fully aware and alive in our amazing human experience.

In the coming months I'll be creating a *Blossom* Facebook platform so that we can keep this conversation going and support each other on our journeys. You will be able to share what's most important to you, honor the love and wins in your life, celebrate and share your creativity, and share what YOU value through your experience. We all need to feel YOUR vibration and connect with YOUR PASSION. The more we talk about, share about, and feel about our life experiences the more we can support this expanding awareness that makes the world a great place to live in and our lives a great place to be in. I can't wait to see what we discover together!

{ create *love*
{ express *beauty* }
be *kind*

All My Love,

be LOVE

Blossom Magazine
is published by
AMY BUTLER LTD

Editor In Chief / Design Director
Amy Butler

Editor / Designer
David Butler

Advertising & Project Manager
Mallory Theiss

Development Coordinator
Sheila Brex

Contributors:
Writing
Molly Lancaster
Amy Flurry
Kim Mettee
Gretel and Steve Adams
Meg Nocero
Monica Lee
Michelle Goldblum
Annie Cacciato

Photography
David Butler
Amy Butler
Lily Glass
Kim Mettee
Sherri Diteman

Styling & location
Monique Keegan
Molly Lancaster

Questions and inquiries to Amy or to
Blossom Magazine can be directed to
blossommagazine@amybutlerdesign.com

Special Thanks!

The creation of *Blossom* has been a major collaborative joy! Each step, each new inspiration has been brought to life with the love, talents, and care of many hands and many hearts. I'd like to share special thanks with these folks who have made this one of the best experiences of my life. I'm so grateful for the opportunity to collaborate with you and have you be an integral part of *Blossom*'s development. I love ya!

Dave Butler, you genius you! Thank you honey for being my partner in love and life. I appreciate all of your gifts and your incredible ability to master photography, graphic design and my giddy requests! The energy and vision in your photography inspires everyone who takes in your images. Thank you for capturing the joy and beauty in all of the stories, in each person. and in every locale. You make everything shine!

My Studio Mates: Lady **Diane Capaci**, you bring the love! Thank you for being such a guiding force for all of us. **Mallory Theiss**, for your sweet focus and powerful ease . . . can I put those two things together? Yes I think I can. You are grace in action and you inspire me always. **Molly Lancaster**, thank you for being such a visionary goddess and for your positive energy and outlook which always translates into yep, I can do it! I really appreciate you. **Sheila Brex**, you are so gorgeous inside! Thank you for mastering the sewing and deadlines and dreams. Thank you for all the care you put into everything you do and the care you give everyone you guide.

My **Friends and Family**, thank you for your unconditional love and support!

Hildie Dunn, my life coach and soul sister. Thank you for your LOVE and guidance and support, for showing me the way to real sustained happiness, and for your beautiful heart that always amazes me . . . and keeps giving more and more. You are a huge gift to me! I'm excited about what's next and to keep the unfolding of my heart going and going.

Patricia Moreno, THANK YOU for bringing your vision to life! IntenSati has changed mine and continues to bring me more joy and abundance in my heart than I could have ever imagined! Thank you for shining your bright and beautiful light on the world and for your courage to be who you really are.

Thank you handwork goddesses for your beautiful sewing, patience, and energy! All of us in the studio are grateful to know you and it's such a pleasure to work alongside you. We celebrate your talents! **Molly Frye, Kerri Thompson, Margaret Moore, Kim Mettee, Beth Huddy, Nichole Redinger, Susan Guzman, Sheila Brex,** and **Colene Sayer.**

Dalyn Dean, Hannah Mugel, Amiti Burkey, Lauren Vannatta, Sarah Gimzer, and **Phil Blundred**. Thank you for modeling and bringing your beautiful smiles and spirit to the magazine! You make the stories come to life!

In celebration of the creative mojo and inspiration from these incredibly talented designers and creators, it has been exciting to include your projects and materials in *Blossom*! The magazine is so much richer and way more fun! Thank you for sharing your gifts!

Patterns and Tutorials:
U-Handbag - Colette Patterns - Jamie Christina Designs - Purl Soho - Interweave Press
www.ruffiesandstuff.com - www.allthingsthrifty.com

Books:
- *Liberty Book of Home Sewing*, Chronicle Books
- *Feminine Wardrobe*, Bunka Publishing Bureau
- Chronicle Books for my how-to books: *In Stitches* and *Style Stitches*

Thank you to our **local friends and businesses** for providing us with incredible support! Our Deven from the Village Flower Basket, Enjoy Co., Granville Millinery, Footloose Vintage Clothing and Taco Dan's, Cat Run Ranch for beautiful flowers for our shoots, The Granville Farmers' Market, Wisp Yarns, and Green Velvet Mercantile.

Monique Keegan of Enjoy Co. for letting us shoot at her gorgeous Summer Haven!

Thank you to all of you for providing us with the best materials to craft, sew & decorate with!
Westminster Fibers - Fairfield - Coats & Clark - Pellon - Stitch Magazine - Chelsea House Design Source
Sew To Speak - Coats Thread - James Thompson Manufacturers - Prym Dritz - Beadsbysandy.com
Sherwin Williams Paints - Springfield Antique Malls - Ikea - West Elm

And to these fine clothiers for their great garments and style!
Anthropology - The Gap - Urban Outfitters - Free People - All Saints - TJ Maxx

Contents

SHINE!

with

Monica Lee

I can't think of a better title for Monica's essay! She is a beacon of love and support. In her call to action she reminds us of why we are here on this planet, of our purpose and of our value. Like me, you will find yourself reading this over and over to continue to glean the wisdom and love that she pours into her writing. I'm going to make sticky notes with her passionate encouragements and post them everywhere! Monica is a most gifted guide and I am very grateful that she shared this special meditation with us. As Monica says "Bring on the beauty, bring on the fun!" ~ Amy

---

What you do matters.

How you show up in life matters. How you respond to life's challenges and bright spots matters.

Here is why I think this...

Have you noticed how dark things have gotten? How entire TV shows are now based on insults and mean criticisms? Have you watched the trailers for movies that feature horror and devastation, all in the name of entertainment? Have you watched the REAL news lately? I don't know what to be more afraid of, new weather patterns or the new political atmosphere in the U.S. There are so many stories of people who are lost, broken, and angry.

If you are bringing joy, creation, beauty into the world in any form, I applaud you. I believe you are an antidote to all the darkness and fear. I would heartily encourage you to keep at it. Keep showing up in your life and the lives of others to counteract what we are exposed to on a daily basis.

Every contribution counts no matter how small. You might be blogging about your life with small children, sharing crafts you do as a family. You never know who it might touch. There may be a young mother who is suffering from postpartum and going to your blog every day may be light at the end of the tunnel. You might be cooking up new recipes, sewing beautiful quilts to be passed down generation to generation - all I can say is, don't stop. We need you. The world needs you.

You might be offering accounting to a new business or you might be the ringleader to a monthly girl's night out. Whatever joy, laughter, and help you are bringing to the planet matters. If you can help another person on the planet get through the day with a smile or with helpful tips or lovely advice, don't think for one second that you don't make a difference.

I recall going through a rough time in my life after 9/11 when I would watch *Sesame Street* with my small son. I would drink my coffee to the sound of "Today is brought to you by the letter J." It put a smile on my face every time. It still does. This day is brought to you by a letter in the alphabet! Who thought of that? Who dipped into their creativity and thought of something so charming? It was better than the news.

Bring on the beauty, bring on the fun!

Don't let anything stop you. Part of being comfortable bringing your personal light into the world is liking and being comfortable with yourself. Don't let the impossible and self-inflicted goal of perfectionism stop you. Thinking that you or anything you do has to be perfect doesn't allow for risk taking and innovation. Don't let other people's criticism and expectations stop you. Gossip and the comparison game is running rampant in today's society. Try your absolute hardest not to participate. Be outspoken about it.
Do it for the self-esteem of the next generation!

Lastly, don't stop yourself. Again and again, I hear people speak badly about themselves. Tackling your inner critic is our generation's final frontier. We put so many limits on ourselves. It is time to work at taking those limits off of ourselves. I am not saying it is an easy task to change the way you see yourself - in fact, I think it can be a daily battle. A battle at first but then it becomes a practice, then a habit - then loving yourself comes as easy as breathing. That is when you are able to shine the brightest.

The example you set by shining bright, by having the courage to bring and create beauty, makes a difference. You are setting the pace for an entire generation that needs you. Bring it on, bring it on! Not for the sake of perfection but for the sake of people. Bring it on, for the sake of counteracting the darkness. Nothing you do is insignificant, and you really were meant to have purpose, to give and to brighten the world around you.
Open your heart to possibilities. - *Monica*

Monica Lee

smartcreativewomen.com

a justaposed study in modern elegance
with my flowy Cameo Voile Fabrics
and the sophisticated interior design
voice of Monique Keegan.

photography by David Butler

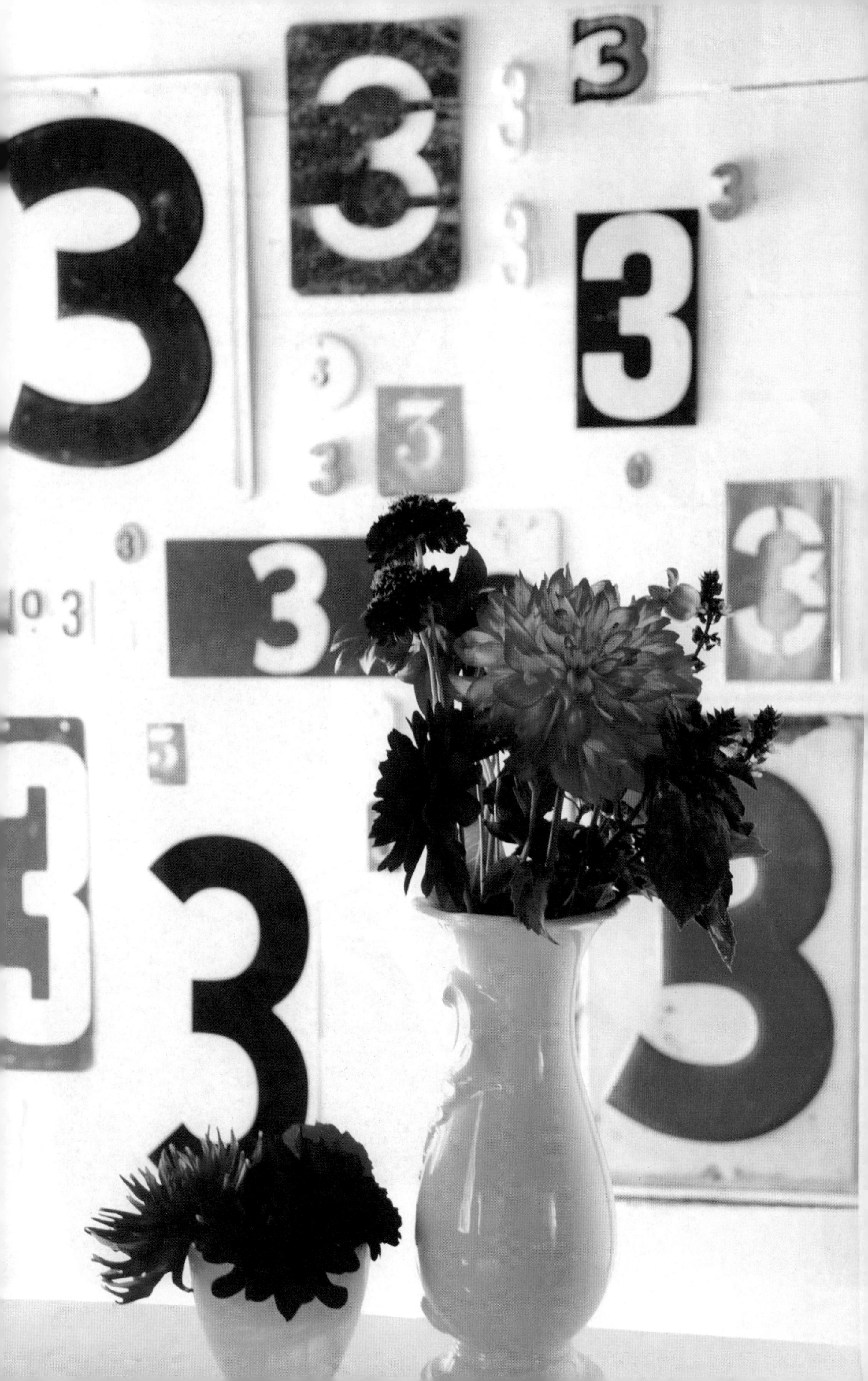
Nº 3

22

Love it? Make it! PAGE Nº220

Love it? Make it! PAGE № 218

Love it? Make it! PAGE Nº 218

WITH PRIVATE BATH

CLEAN

RIFTED COAL
SUPPLY CO.

THE LEAP

taken by

Michelle Goldblum

It is such a thrill to look at your life and see the connecting pieces that allowed you to cross paths with someone you are just "supposed to know." Michelle is one of those very special people for me. We met at the Omega Institute in Rhinebeck, NY a year and a half ago at an IntenSati retreat, a weekend that transformed the life of everyone who attended. Michelle's journey over this past year is a massive inspiration! It's been powerful for me to witness her honesty and wholehearted commitment to taking each step toward her dream. It's been amazing to watch the magic unfold as she embraces the changes in her life knowing that she is exactly where she needs to be and encourages us to know that we can let go and tune inward and connect with who we really are, love and perfection. Thank you Michelle! You are one big bright beautiful light! ~ Amy

---

If my life story

was already written and bound, it would be pretty hard to miss.
My book would be big and bright. Perpendicular patterns and Crayola candy colors would splash the pages. Magentas, salmons, limes, and aquas. Checkers, rainbows, bubbles. Zigs and zags.
All different textures, shapes and sensations coming together beautifully. Making a beautiful whole.
Making a perfect story.

The years will show what the days never could.

Up until the last year or so, I had been living within a single pixel of my pixelated masterpiece.
I had forgotten that I was on a path, and that every single moment, every single choice, every single decision, every single everything that was happening was leading me to exactly where I was supposed to be. I forgot that although I was the star in this incredible work of art, it wasn't me who was holding the brush. This is a story about what happened when I took a step out of the pixel, remembered the truth, and began to trust the work of the artist.

A year ago this summer, I was living a life that looked completely different than the one I have now. I was living in the Upper West Side of Manhattan, in an apartment that I owned. I was the advertising account lead of 2 multi-million-dollar pharmaceutical accounts. I was living with my boyfriend of 3 years and with his children every other weekend. I knew who I was in this world and truly had a full life. But something wasn't right. I knew it deep in my belly, yet refused to acknowledge it in my mind for a very long time. This life of mine, it just wasn't right. Then one day, my identity broke.

When the student is ready, the teacher will appear.
Buddhist Proverb

I finally admitted to myself that my boyfriend and I just weren't fitting together anymore. The weekend he packed his boxes, I left the city and escaped to Omega Institute in Rhinebeck, NY to attend a weekend-long IntenSati retreat. I arrived on the campus broken, numb, without a solid sense of who I was or how I would even introduce myself. An empty vessel. I arrived without any expectations or even an understanding of why I was there, other than to get my mind off of the U-Haul van outside of my building.

Perhaps it was because of the honesty and love of the women around me that weekend. Or maybe it was due to the beauty of the nature that ensconced me, or the vegan deliciousness that revitalized me. It could have been the positive affirmations that we yelled together, or the tears that we cried, or the unconditional acceptance that we gave and received. Whatever the reason, I woke up. I suddenly awakened to the obvious, undeniable fact that this was all supposed to happen. This relationship, this painful ending, this was all perfect. And not only were the experiences perfect, I myself was perfect. Life was working out exactly as it should, and every single choice I had made up until that moment - every yes and every no, every time I moved forward and every time I held back - it all was perfect. There were no rights or wrongs. There were no mistakes, no such thing as time wasted. It all had led me to that second at Omega,
where I woke up.

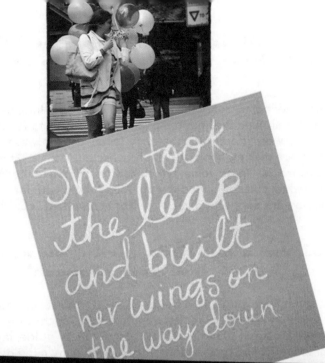

She took the leap and built her wings on the way down

photography provided by Michelle Goldblum

YOUR JOURNEY HAS MOLDED YOU FOR YOUR GREATER GOOD, AND IT WAS EXACTLY WHAT IT NEEDED TO BE. DON'T THINK THAT YOU'VE LOST TIME. IT TOOK EACH AND EVERY SITUATION YOU HAVE ENCOUNTERED TO BRING YOU TO THE NOW. AND NOW IS RIGHT ON TIME.

-ASHA TYSON-

We must be willing to get rid of the life we've planned, so as to have the life that is waiting for us.
Joseph Campbell

Everything changed. I got home from Omega and started to take IntenSati classes every day. I began to eat organic foods and continued writing in the journal I started at the retreat. I surrounded myself with like-minded people who were living lives that they loved, or who were doing everything in their power to do so. People who were making happiness their conscious choice. As my community grew around me, I began to tune inward. My inner voice, which had once been limited to to-do lists and commercial jingles, was suddenly loud, consistent, and loving. And I knew without a doubt that she had always been there, loving me, supporting me. It was only now that I could hear her so clearly.

"Good morning, little girl! You are so pretty! I love you so much!"

I listened to her and let her guide me. I believed her; I trusted her and I checked in with her about everything and anything. What do I really want to eat for lunch? How should I respond to my boss? Should I walk down this street or the next one? I let my inner guide, my higher self, become my GPS system. I let go of the reins and trusted her choices, even if my mind disagreed or didn't understand. I stopped seeing things as happening to me, and instead, saw everything was happening FOR me. When I learned that an IntenSati retreat that I had saved up for and signed up for in Mexico was canceled, I found myself excited to see why. Just 2 days later (2 days!!) I received a "Living Social" voucher in my inbox advertising an 8-day trip to India, round trip flights from NYC included, just $500 more and 7 days after the Mexico trip was scheduled to depart. I accepted the obvious push from the universe, traveled to India by myself, and from that point forward, everything began to unfold extraordinarily quickly.

Leap, and the net will appear.
John Burroughs

I returned from India and stopped eating meat. Through a series of coincidences (note: there are no coincidences!) I found the Oneness Meditation community and became a Oneness blessing giver. Oneness is the belief that we are all connected. That while we happen to be in these bodies right now, the truth is that we are all just energy, and that energy is love. We are all just love energy, walking around in these vehicles that we identify with, that we name. Mine is named Michelle. Oneness Meditation taught me how to tune in to that energy, to that truth. I learned how to fill myself up with this incredible feeling of bliss and love whenever I wanted. I saw that all of us, from the homeless man on the sidewalk to the bird chirping outside my window to the baby crying next door, we are all the same. I began to love everyone and everything. One by one, I forgave all those that had hurt me or caused me pain. I forgave them, and I loved them. I gave them the love that they so obviously needed. I saw that hurt people, hurt people. I stopped taking things personally.

Spread the love. BE the love. See the love.

Once I was living a life where I recognized that I was love, and that I was supposed to love, and that life was supposed to be good, magic happened. Miracles started appearing. Life became easy and fluid. My inner voice became my only voice.

Within 2 weeks of realizing I needed to sell my apartment to release myself of the weight of the mortgage, it was sold. Within 2 months of knowing I needed to leave my corporate pharmaceutical career to help people spread messages of positivity and awareness, I co-founded my company, I AM. creative. Within 2 months of launching, we have an incredible client list and are working on some major, transformational national events in the mind/body/spirit space. My brilliant partner, Audrey, and I met in Oneness Meditation, giving love energy to each other. I live in the East Village in a cozy, delicious walk-up. I am living a life of love. I am surrounded every day by loving people, who are loving people. It is a life beyond what I could have ever imagined for myself. It is a life that continues to surprise me and entertain me with its synchronicities and twists and turns.

My advice is simple. Let go. Let go of the reins and tune inward. You are exactly where you are supposed to be, and every single millisecond of your life has led you to right now, reading these words. You already know the answers. You are love, and you are *absolutely perfect*.

Michelle Goldblum is the co-founder of I AM. creative, a brand strategy, development and marketing firm specializing in the mind/body/spirit space. You can reach her via facebook and twitter.

"QUOTATION" SPARKS

behind the words with

Meg Nocero

I believe magic is everywhere and people cross our paths for a reason. In just such an incidence I have had the pleasure of meeting Margaret Nocero. We have never met in person but I feel like I've known her forever. As I began curating content for the magazine her writings came into my life via a mutual friend who shared one of Meg's Thoughts of the Day. I didn't even hesitate, I instantly sent Meg an email asking to connect and crossed my fingers that she'd be interested in my sharing her beautiful writings in *Blossom*. You will understand what I mean as you experience her work.

In Meg's own words she explains how she has taken heartfelt steps toward her dream.
"I started on a journey over a year ago to identify and live my purpose in this world. There is actually a bit of history behind my words - my mom passed away from cancer in April of 2011. We had beautiful conversations each morning before I started work that left me truly inspired. When she died, the grief was terrible. A friend suggested I dedicate a time each day to connect to her - my thoughts of the day are my connections with her - I take the inspiration and love I got from her and share with others who may want to hear it and I get to feel close to my mom. I have written now over 100 thoughts of the day since I started and it has helped me heal."

Meg's words will totally inspire you! Every time I open one of Meg's writings it is "just what I needed to see" that day. Divine timing? I think so. Meg is currently working on publishing her first book called *The Beauty Within - A Soul Talk Inspired by My Mother - A Handbook of Inspirations*. I will look forward to adding her book to my library. Thank you Meg for sharing your amazing gifts! To learn more about Meg and connect with her wisdom and heart daily, please visit www.megnocero.wordpress.com ~ Amy

Rock bottom
became
the solid foundation
on which
I rebuilt my life.

J.K. Rowling, novelist

We all grow spiritually as a result of many different life events. Some of the most profound instances of growth in my life have come as a result of necessity because of loss, dissatisfaction with life circumstance, or feelings of helplessness. It is in these moments or experiences that I have discovered who is supporting me and I have discovered what I am made of. While transformation in life may be difficult when you resist it because of fear of the unknown, sometimes when you get to the point where you feel that you are at the end of the rope and ignoring change is no longer an option - that is when you hit rock bottom with only one way to go - UP!

I love J.K. Rowling's approach to the lowest time in her life: she turned inward to her core, she looked within for her answers and guidance. And this turning toward herself with love has proven to establish for her a solid foundation to build her own legacy of love. What came from that time in her life was a beautiful tribute to the magic of the human spirit and the magic and beauty of life as she authored the Harry Potter series. Each day is an opportunity to continue to build on your strong foundation, keep building on your belief in yourself - and belief in your own uniqueness. As you do this, you continue to build on the foundation that will be your legacy of love to the world. Turning something that felt like the end of the world into a new beginning is the gift we get as each new day starts. AS long as we do our best in this regard, we cannot be considered fake or a hypocrite. AS long as we continue to act upon our own guidance and incorporate our actions with love, ours will be a legacy of leadership based upon solid principles. You cannot do better than that on your way up!

~ Meg Nocero

Personal transformation can and does have global effects. As we go, so goes the world, for the world is us. The revolution that will save the world is ultimately a personal one.

Marianne Williamson, author, lecturer, and founder of The Peace Alliance

I adore Mondays. How is that for a "shift" statement? Mondays have always been a day of possibility for me, the start of a new week and the beginning of a fresh clean slate. Mondays are perfect days to declare to yourself that you are going to acknowledge your own personal growth and conscious transformation in your life. While the caterpillar becomes a beautiful butterfly - we do not witness each and every step that it takes to create such a magnificent creature. The caterpillar just surrenders and believes in the process. And we, as a part of nature, witness the miraculous butterfly that is the result of the work. The same goes for all of us. While we truly do not witness each moment of transformation each day as we set out into the world, all the work that we put into ourselves is a part of the process that goes into creating the beautiful creatures that we are. If we do the inner and outer work and surrender to the process, we transform into a better and more amazing version of ourselves and, by doing so, the world can't help but become a more beautiful place. I love the idea that our own personal transformation can have global impact. When we mix in the ingredients of kindness, love, joy, faith, and laughter, one person has the chance to make a mark on the world starting on a small scale.

On this auspicious day, I challenge all of you to surrender to the process and feel the positive transformation entering your life. Call your angels, whether spiritual or physical, to guide you if you need some assistance or serve as an angel to another yourself. Never give up on yourself and your path because you may just be that close to the effortless movement toward realizing a dream that can have a global impact for many. And when you embrace the change in your life and encourage others to do the same, you are liberated from the dictates of a stagnant society and the shift has begun. We are all personally responsible to do our part to join the revolution of change simply by acting on our own enthusiastic and optimistic belief in ourselves and the world. Then you can truly experience the butterfly effect of life. With a flap of your wings, the positive energy you release travels and is shared by more people than you will ever know. When you go out of your way to do better on a daily basis with an attitude of love, kindness, and gratitude, you can make a difference in the world as you become a warrior of love, courage, and peace, for in reality the world is only a mirror of each one of us. I will choose today to see its reflection of inner and outer beauty transforming into my own reality, will you?

~ Meg Nocero

Since love grows within you, so beauty grows. For love is the beauty of the soul.

St. Augustine

In today's world, the majority of people are often too consumed with worry about how they are perceived by others basing their determination solely on the outside appearance. Unfortunately, our focus is often misplaced. While we can decorate our faces and our bodies with clothes, makeup, and material things, we will never fully step into our true beauty until we make a proactive intention to give love to ourselves and others. When we shift our focus from the external to the internal, we will start to truly understand our purpose here. It is the beauty within that emanates for all to see. It is the beauty within that needs to be nurtured. It is the beauty within that we must take care to cultivate. It is the beauty within that makes us the special and unique person that we were created to be. When you shift your focus, the world starts to make more sense and our experiences become more and more like blessings rather than hardships. The beauty within grows when we focus on feelings of love. We are all here in this life to make connections with others coming from a place of complete love. If you shift to the internal and focus on the love in your heart, you get to know your life with a renewed sense of zeal and enthusiasm. When you come from the perspective of love on the inside, you will get the best makeover on the outside and not even have to pay the big bucks for it.

For love is truly the beauty of the soul!

~ Meg Nocero

There are days which occur in this climate, at almost any
season of the year, wherein the world reaches its perfection,
when the air, the heavenly bodies, and the earth, make a
harmony, as if nature would indulge her offspring; when,
in these bleak upper sides of the planet, nothing is to desire
that we have heard of the happiest latitudes, and we bask in
the shining hours of Florida and Cuba; when everything that
has life gives signs of satisfaction, and the cattle that lie
on the ground seem to have great and tranquil thoughts.
These halcyons may be looked for with a little more
assurance in that pure October weather, which we
distinguish by the name of

INDIAN SUMMER

- Ralph Waldo Emerson

photography by David & Amy Butler

{ You can't stop the waves,
but you can learn to surf }

Jon Kabat-Zinn

LIVE IN THE MOMENT

Love it? Make it! PAGE № 218 № 221

"Because there's nothing more beautiful than the way the ocean refuses to stop kissing the shoreline, no matter how many times it's sent away."
-Sarah Kay

73

"All matter, including you and I, has rhythmic movement within it and our quest should be to create a proper rhythmic harmony within ourselves... you feel happy when you sit near an ocean because your vibrations try to synchronize with the frequency of the waves."

- Ed Viswanathan

TAKING ROOT

growing the dream of

Sunny Meadows Flower Farm

The blossoming, serendipitous vision of Gretel and Steve Adams
to create a fully organic flower farm from scratch.
Just down the road in Columbus, OH.

photography by David & Amy Butler

We really do consider ourselves serendipitous farmers. Neither of
us went to school for it and we both grew up in suburbia. Steve
had an apprenticeship at Anderson Orchards (a flower farm despite
the name), which sparked our passion for farming. And I, Gretel,
was blessed enough to inherit a 10 acre lot in Columbus that my father
bought in the '80s. We both love to be outside in the dirt and
to be more connected with nature, and every year we are trying new
things, seeing how it will work as a cut flower in our production.

We try to live life as sustainably as possible by using organic practices, canning
the food we grow, composting to make our own soil amendments, and heating
our house with wood, among other things. We make soap, salve, and herbal tea
mixes for sale, which keeps us busy through the winter. Winter is also spent
reading and attending farming conferences as well as touring other farms so that we
can gain from other people's knowledge. Being a part of the Association of
Specialty Cut Flower Growers has been a big help; it's a great community of
growers nationwide who are always willing to guide you in the right direction.

We see ourselves as advocates for local flowers, explaining to
people where their flowers come from if they aren't local, and
the global floral industry they are buying into. We enjoy farming,
but most of all we enjoy spreading the flowery joy into
other people's lives! That's why we like providing flowers for green
weddings so much, because you get to be a part of a very
special day and help the bride execute her vision. We always say
that food may feed the body, but flowers feed the soul!

- Gretel & Steve Adams

79

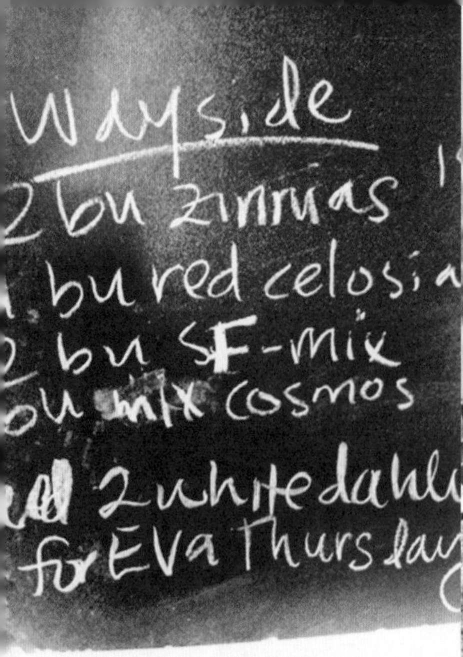

Wayside
2 bu zinnias
1 bu red celosia
2 bu SF-mix
bu mix cosmos

2 white dahlia
for Eva Thursday

FARMHAND

Sunny Meadows
Flower Farm
at Market!

The orchestra of color and texture comes
alive at one of Sunny Meadows'
bountiful flower stands at the
Granville Farmers' Market!

Mixed
Bouquets
$12/20

Sunny Meadows

Lilie
$10/

Soap $5
or 5 for $20
Salve $4

a Flower Farm

🌸 Columbus OH

www.oursunnymeadows.com

Zinni
7/

never lose your sense of

WONDER

photography by David & Amy Butler

featuring fresh ideas in laminate fabrics...

"YOUTH IS HAPPY
BECAUSE IT HAS
THE CAPACITY TO
SEE BEAUTY.
ANYONE WHO KEEPS
THE ABILITY TO
SEE BEAUTY NEVER
GROWS OLD."
- FRANZ KAFKA -

Love it? Make it! PAGE №229

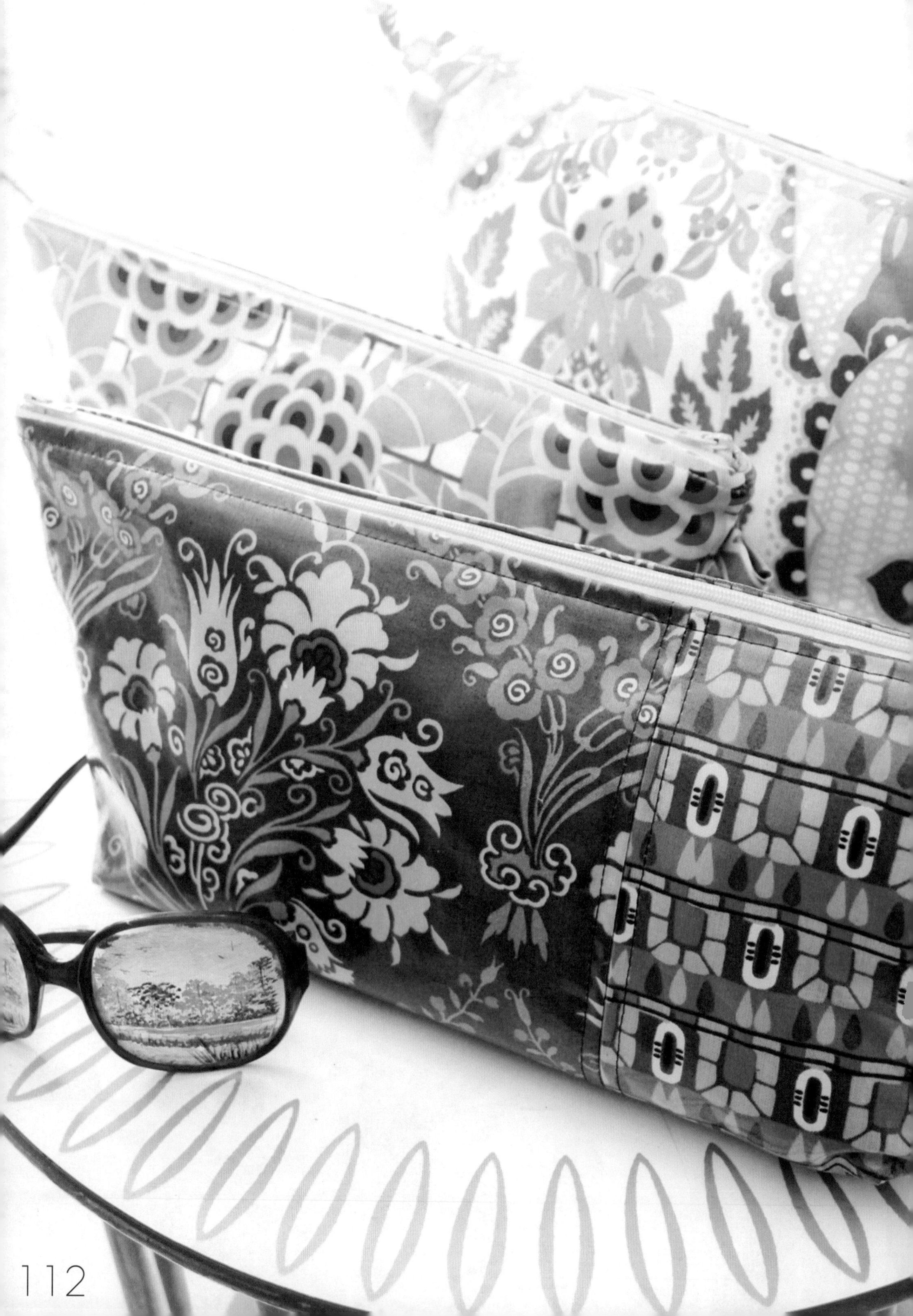

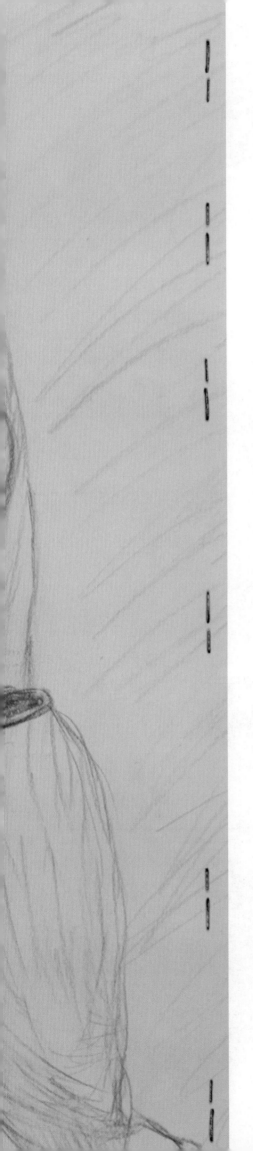

Beautiful Minds

empowering creative exploration at

Granville Studio of Visual Arts

In 2007, two women armed only with knowledge, love, and passion launched an experimental non-profit, after-school arts program for young people that has become a national benchmark in quality creativity education.

story by **Annie Cacciato**
self-portraits by **students of GSVA**

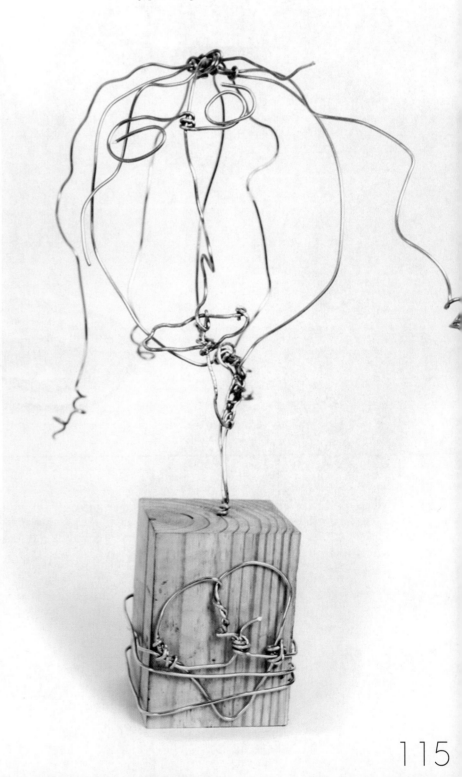

When my family and I moved from California to Ohio nine years ago, a new chapter in my life began. My husband Matt and I wanted to raise our three girls closer to our family. A few years later, upon enrolling our middle daughter, Grace, in preschool, I met Kerry Dixon. Kerry would become my best friend and the co-founder of GSVA.

Kerry and I shared a love of art. As we became closer, we shared discussions and opinions on creativity, imagination, the arts, and art education. Together we exposed our five girls, Nicole, Grace, JoJo, Ruby, and Lulu to beautiful art, creative art classes, and music. During this time, we made a conscious effort to observe their individual learning styles and creative growth. We observed how each of our daughters embraced creativity and the art mediums in a unique way.

We both understood the importance of individual courage in the creative learning process. It was very clear to us that one way and one size did not fit all children. We became increasingly interested in what role creativity played in public education.

Armed with our personal knowledge and curiosity, we began to research the priorities of 21st century public education. We were alarmed to discover that while education leaders around the world deeply valued creative thinking and development, the reality was that the current United States education system did not align with those values. Creativity, the arts, and individual creative development were not priorities in most schools. Budget cuts continuously caused art classes to be eliminated from the school day in many cities and this trend continues. School districts with art tend to prioritize the art discipline and technique, rather than the mental process and the development of the student's creative thinking.

Kerry and I asked many questions. Why weren't imagination, curiosity, creativity, ideas, and dreams included in the core education process? How will our girls, and children everywhere, learn to be creative thinkers and doers in the current system? We wanted to change the current system to include the creative process as a foundational component of education.

So, one December morning in 2007, we decided to launch an innovative non-profit organization dedicated to creativity and life-long learning. With a seed of an idea, passion for our purpose, and a vision for change, we decided to put our ideas into action. With open hearts and minds, the love of our families, and a small but strong support network, Kerry and I began our journey. In March of 2008, GSVA was born, a creative education non-profit.

Five years later, after thousands of hours of love, sweat, and tears, here we stand. Through the years, countless volunteers and a team of the most creative professionals and visionary educators I know joined us. We have seen our girls grow up into amazingly creative individuals. Our families, and especially my husband Matt for me, have been a wonderful support system thus far, and will surely continue to be. Today, GSVA is a national leader in quality creative education experiences for schools, community and business organizations, families, and individuals. Kerry and I are so blessed to have been on this purposeful journey.

Today, we invite you to prioritize and learn more about the creative process in your life and in your community.

Recently, we created a scholarship program for at-risk teens called the Sunflower Connection. This program is intended to broaden the horizons of young women at risk and empower them to think creatively. As a daughter of a broken home with a wonderful loving mother and an absent father, I am empathetic to all children who have dealt with emotional and physical trauma in their lives. As a survivor of a serious car accident in which I experienced a life-changing head injury, I have personal experience with trauma. My accident played a major role in my level of empathy and understanding for young women at risk.

This is my personal experience that drives my passion and commitment to our at-risk program, Sunflower Connection. Every one of these at-risk girls is hungry for a way to feed their soul, to develop an ounce of courage, and to feel the support of real people that believe in the possibilities of who they may become.

GSVA has changed my life, but not mine alone. It has shaped the lives of my daughters, Kerry's daughters, our families, students, teachers, employees, volunteers, collaborators, and the list goes on. While the arts and the creative process are still not a part of the regular school day in most schools, GSVA provides a steady alternative. Our goals of broadening horizons and educating children in creativity and the arts continue to be realized each day, and will be more so through the Sunflower Connection. We have designed quality curriculum and consulting programs for GSVA, but we hope to spread the philosophy of GSVA and the Sunflower Connection throughout the country in order to make sure that people learn how to think creatively and imaginatively.

Annie Cacciato
Co-founder of GSVA, Granville Studio of Visual Arts
www.gsvaonline.org

HISTORY

{ GENERATIONS OF COLLECTING AND CRAFT }

WRITTEN BY AMY BUTLER

PHOTOGRAPHY BY DAVID & AMY BUTLER

PHOTOS OF MY MOTHER AND GREAT-GRANDMOTHER MURIEL

I love this story. We are so naturally molded by our family heritage. It's wonderful to celebrate all of the positive ways we are gifted by our family experience. I find the things that I love, foods, colors, artwork, crafts, collections, etc. are all inspired by the interests and passions of my parents and grandparents. I believe I was meant to be an artist and I also know that the way I see the world has been greatly influenced by my mother and grandmother. I find myself collecting the same things, decorating in similar ways, and making art with a familiar hand. I love this feeling because it gives me a great deal of comfort. I feel loved, supported, and eternally connected to them via our shared interests. Looking back it all makes so much sense, doesn't it? My grandmother Velma taught me how to sew at a young age and her home as well as my Mom's was always bustling with some sort of handmade something going on - macramé, quilting, sewing, knitting, dried flower arranging - you name it! That's also how they decorated their homes - with what they made and what they collected at garage sales and auctions. Now some 40+ years later I fall more deeply in love with my family and am so grateful for what they've given me. My beloved G continues to inspire me even though she's passed on. I feel her nudges and know she is thrilled to see me using her silk tie flying geese quilt blocks that she lovingly pieced together by hand. They are the inspiration for the mini flying geese quilt project and pillow. I love you too G! And I keep G's artifacts all around me. Her beautiful English Coal and Port dishes are featured in the photographs along with the full size bed quilt she left for me. I inherited my Mom's drawing skills and her passion for natural treasures and found trinkets - all waiting to be made into something, I think jewelry, but the time spent in beautiful dishes just as they are gives me oodles of inspiration and a sense of awe for the natural gifts that surround me. Mom and me on nature hikes identifying birds, picking up rocks, feathers and shells - something we still do together as often as we can, gives me so much joy and comfort. These experiences connect me to what's really valuable in my life and has afforded me a bulging collection of found items that have a life of their own displayed in my cherry cabinet in the living room. When I open the doors for a fix, I'm transported back to all of the great memories and experiences.

The pink shoebox is my family photo album! I had to place it here and share it with you. It's falling apart from all the rooting and sorting that commenced with it over the years. Every time I'd visit G I had to get "the box" out! I'd lose myself in memories and imaginings of earlier days. It was my only link to my past. I still keep the shoebox handy and don't think I can pull myself to sorting out the box into proper photo albums. Something special would be lost. I may step up a bit and play with filing a few special pics in my Memory Keeper folios. Something you may enjoy doing with your special pics.

In G's honor and my Mom's, I included a painted gourd project {very '70s I know} but aren't they super cool?! They remind me of sophisticated ceramics. I think G would approve! Of course you can paint amazing patterns and colors on them too. I wanted to create a more subtle feel so they would mesh beautifully with Monique's Summer Haven Camp interior. The quilt projects are an homage to Velma and the silhouettes are there as a nod to our past. I hope this piece inspires you to explore your family history and play with some of the inspirations you've gleaned from your experiences and turn them into expressions of passion and love. Have fun! ~ XO Amy

121

MY GRANDMA VELMA'S
FLYING GEESE SILK TIE
PATCHES & EPHEMERA

Flying Geese
Silk tie Quilt Patches

1783

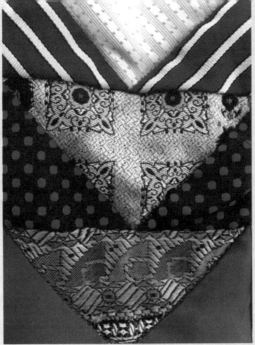

Love it? Make it! PAGE Nº221

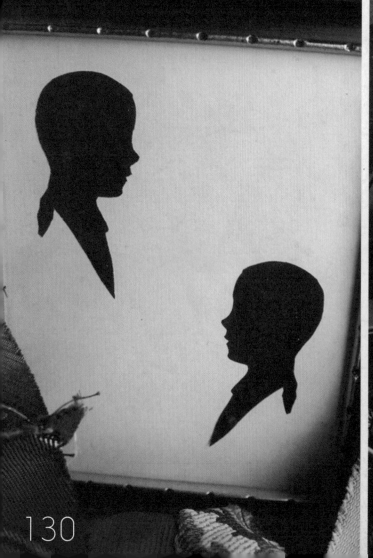

from
NATURAL

Love it? Make it! PAGE Nº 218

COLOUR  STORIES

inspirations from jewelry designer and colorist

Kim Mettee

It's an honor to introduce you to "my Kim" and have her share her journey with
you. We have been soul sisters for a very long time, truly two peas in a
pod! We get giddy about anything that has to do with creating, collecting,
curating, and colour! Our special friendship is ignited by our passion for
expression and our willingness to nurture each other's hearts through many years
of change and growth. She is a beautiful talent who inspires all with her
rich intensity and appreciation for life. I am blessed to see the world through
her eyes and am thrilled that she will touch your life today too! ~ Amy

photography by Kim Mettee & David Butler

an introduction to the visual book

COLOUR by STORIES
Kim Mettee

Inspiration. Interpretation. Exploration. Lovingly created.

Each of us has a story to tell. We have collected fragments over time . . . elements
that reflect who we are as individuals. And when we take the time to
really "SEE" what we've gathered, a colourful story begins to unfold.
Colour Stories is about inspiration, interpretation, and exploration. It is a
visual narrative for not only myself to enjoy but for others as well. I wanted
to create a photo journal as a way to bring everything together that
inspires me as an artist. I used collage as a way to organize the myriad
photographs I have taken over the years, not only my own work, i.e.,
my jewelry and paintings, but also beautiful vignettes featuring my collections
of antique and tribal textiles, rocks, stones, sundry natural and fibrous
bits such as seed pods and beach debris, for which the eclectic has been
given rhythm and rhyme. My spirited eye is always guided to
celebrate flowers via photo-documentation and thus in addition to this
reoccurring theme, so too are the decorative tins and nifty containers that
house many of the beads and raw materials used to create my art.
These are some of the elements that surround me and inspire me daily.

Colour Stories sprang from a quiet and reflective place. My father was very ill at the time,
and as a secondary caregiver, I found myself often drained and overwhelmed at the
beginning and at the end of each day. In order to free myself from the grueling and
emotional hold this intense experience was having on me, I knew I needed to create
a place where I could go to feel nurtured and released from my suffering. Just simply to
escape wasn't mindful enough. Without any preconceived notions, I dove into the
meticulous process of gathering, sorting, and arranging hundreds of photographs of
my colourful life. I was grateful for the beautiful catharsis which was to unfold.

Feeling raw, exposed vulnerability which revealed the magnificence of my vision.
There is something so tangible and delicious about tapping into one's
source of light and knowing. I felt a flow of extreme happiness coursing through my
veins, not unlike the warm transfusion of hemoglobin my father required often to
restore his energy. I poured over and into the pages I laid out, shuffling contours with
textures, patterns with light and shape and colour . . . completely mesmerizing.
As the seconds merged into minutes into hours and days, I felt more oxygen in my
lungs and my fatigue was replaced with wide awakeness. Such focus and meditation
had been rejuvenating. Seeing my meaningful life strewn across the pages in a
patchwork-like quilt, filled me with great pride and satisfaction.
"This is my soul on these pages" I said to myself.

What had been revealed was the powerful manifestation of a purposeful and loving action.
Colour Stories fulfilled a desire to visually funnel and refine my beautiful sensibilities in a way
that could be easily communicated and understood without words. A sense of tranquility
washed over me and an eagerness to share this treasury with the world consumed every
fiber of my being. I was overcome with gratitude for simply . . . being ME. How each of us sees
the world is based on what inspires us, how we interpret that inspiration and the explorative
path we choose. If you wish to share your colour stories, or reach out to me with curiosity,
I welcome all inquiries and I invite you to visit me at the site below! ~ Kim

KIMMETTEEDESIGNS.COM

"I was overcome with gratitude for simply...being ME."

COLOURSTORIES

Inspiration..Interpretation..Exploration

designed and lovingly created by kim mettee

"I was overcome with gratitude for simply...being ME."

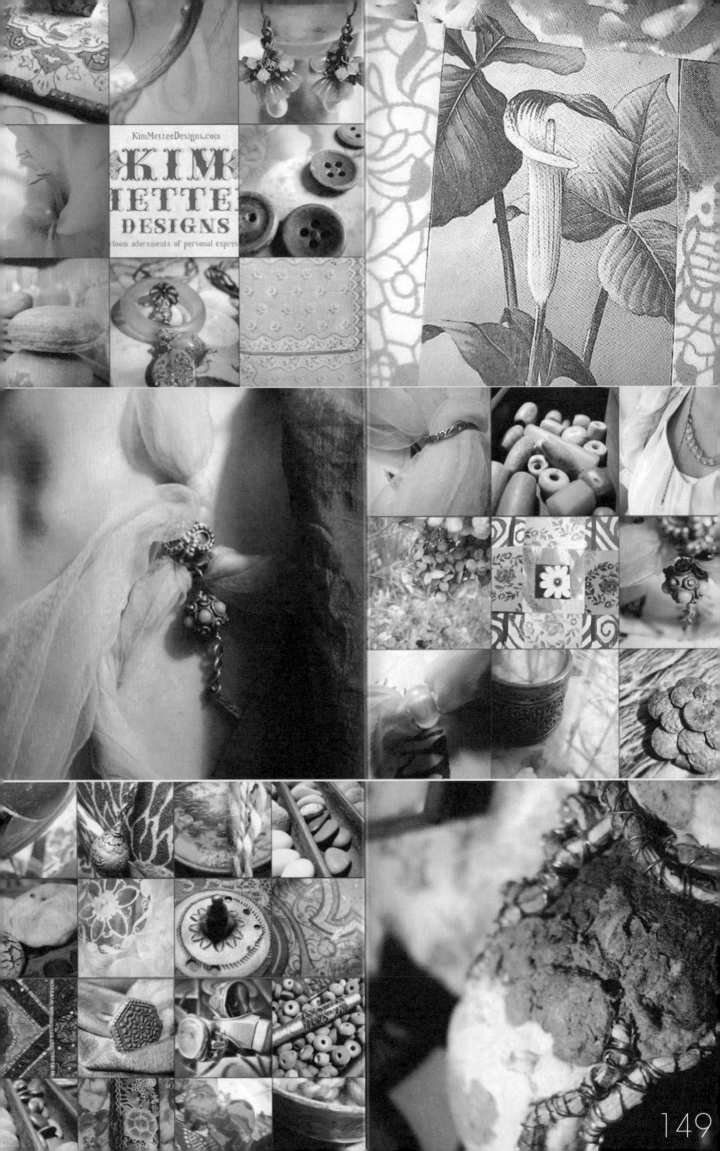

PURCHASED FROM

Mighty Hand

vintage

STYLED FOR YOU IN
COLUMBUS OHIO

OLD SOUL

photography by Lily Glass
written by Molly Lancaster

Husband and wife artists
Molly & Brandon Lancaster's
Mighty Hand Vintage
is a fresh new voice in vintage
style for fashion & home.
By finding Old Soul in
the beautifully utilized,
Mighty Hand is turning
their unique vision into
an American dream.

MOLLY & BRANDON met while working together at Abercrombie & Fitch (Molly on the textile team and Brandon on the graphics team). As their friendship grew into a relationship, Molly decided to take on a new job as Amy Butler's design assistant. This opened her eyes to the small business world of design - observing & learning from a couple who have created a life together around their talents & what they love. This is what propelled Molly and Brandon into a new creative venture.

"It's all about complimenting each other - balancing one another as designers AND in our day to day life. Inspiring and encouraging each other as artists and human beings - they are so intertwined - you can't have one without the other! The best thing about creating a brand with your life partner is it seems to remove a bit of fear. You're in it together and no matter what decisions you make - good or bad - you have each other's support and trust and commitment and that is such a freeing feeling!" - *Molly Lancaster*

vintage

Mighty Hand

made
modern

157

vintage

Mighty Hand

made modern

PACIFICA

**EXOTIC AND ROMANTIC
INSPIRATIONS
LEAP FROM THE PAGES OF A
TRAVEL SKETCHBOOK**

featuring my CAMEO fabrics

photography by David Butler

Love it? Make it! PAGE № 222

Love it? Make it! PAGE Nº 232

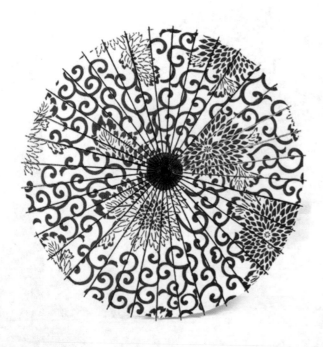

est la couleur
es rêves.

Love it? Make it! PAGE Nº 222

Love it? Make it! PAGE Nº 222

Love it? Make it! PAGE №223

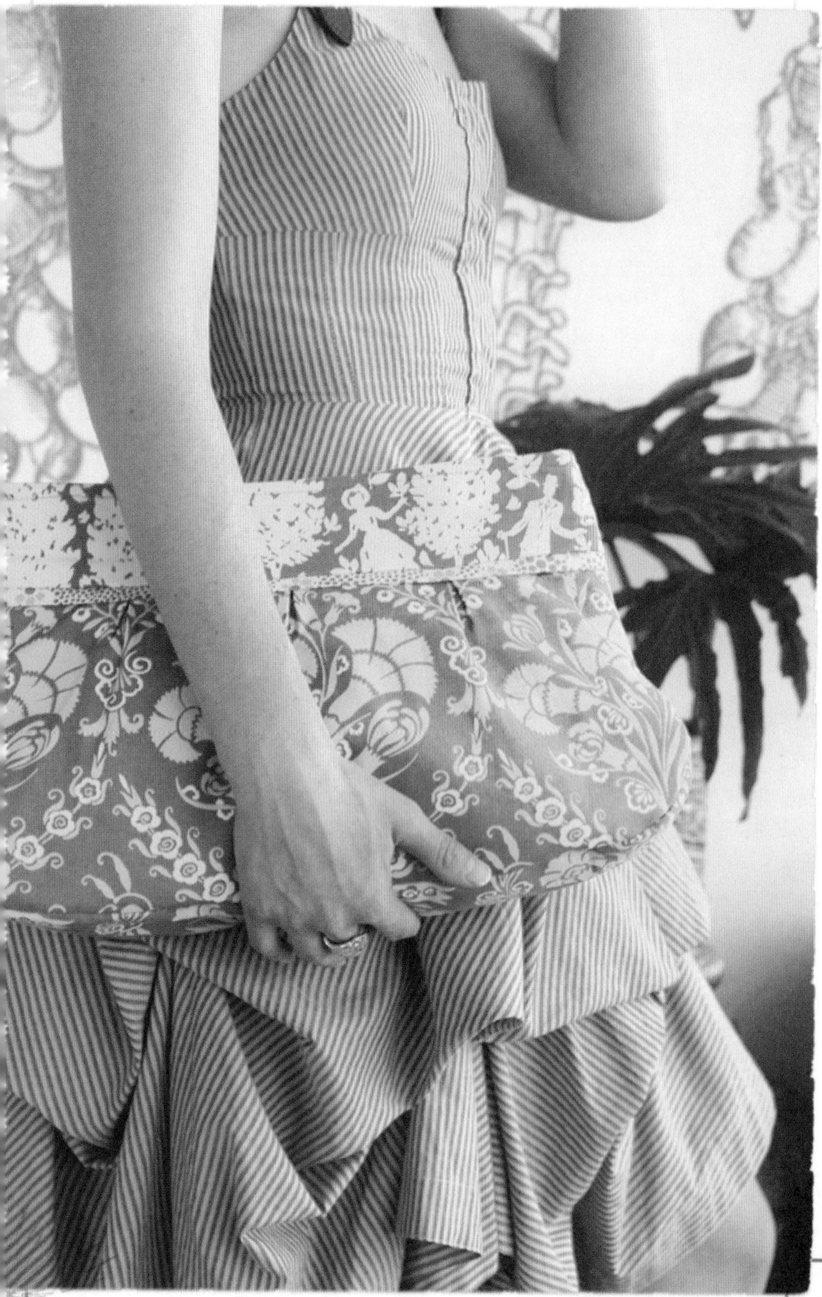

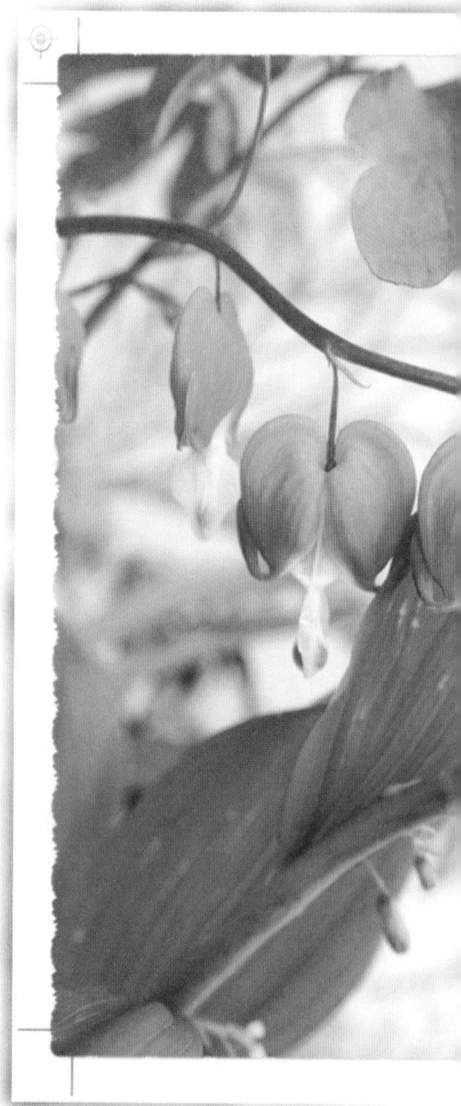

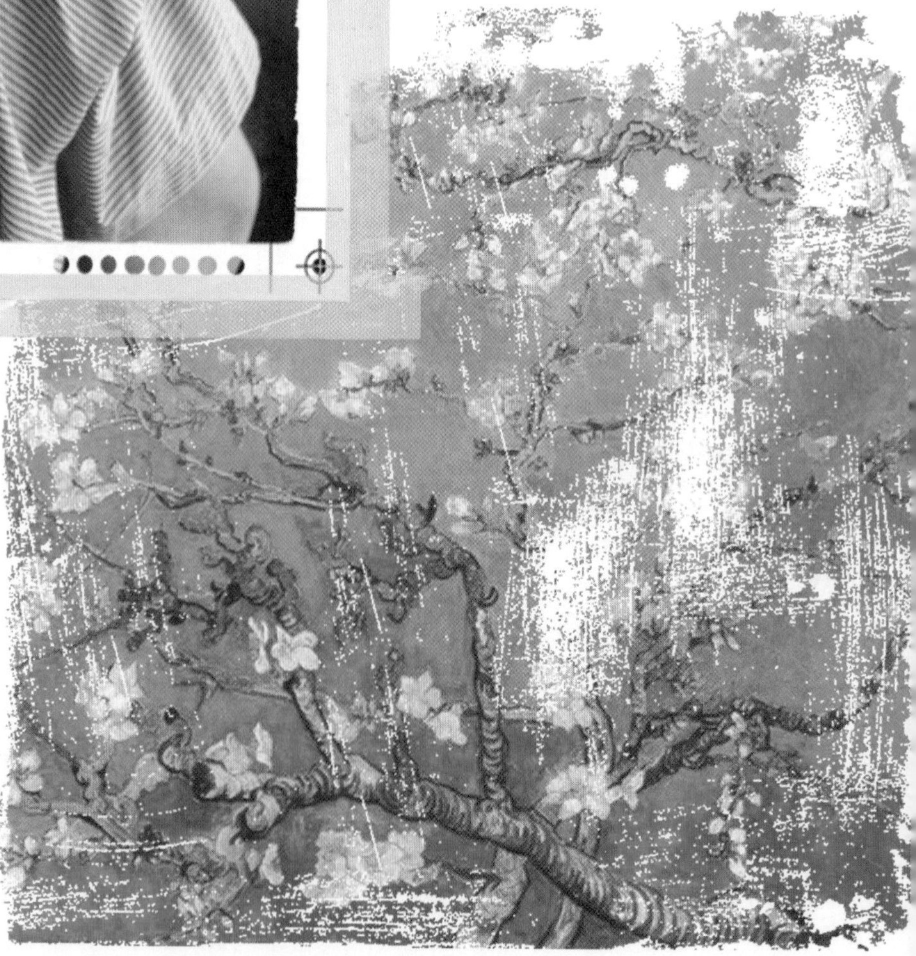

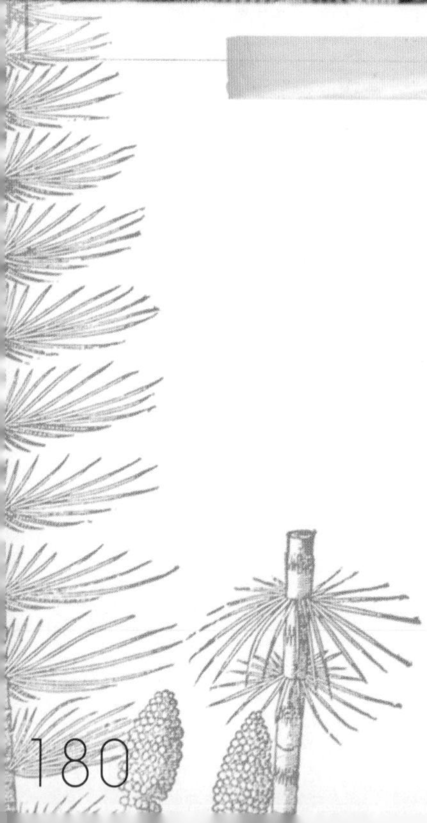

The Right Mix

Amy Flurry's

Recipe for Press
book signing & chat at Portland, Oregon's lovely

Beam & Anchor Boutique
owned & operated by Jocelyn & Robert Rahm and Currie Person

In one version of the new startup economy, longtime magazine editor Amy Flurry is empowering entrepreneurs by giving them the tools, insider know-how, and confidence to share their works and get press. Along the way, her story blossomed.

story by Amy Flurry
photography by Sherri Diteman

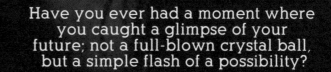

Have you ever had a moment where
you caught a glimpse of your
future; not a full-blown crystal ball,
but a simple flash of a possibility?

For 18 years, I contributed to some of the most popular magazines
on the newsstands - giving voice to emerging designers,
independent labels, chefs, and smaller brands all vying to be
the next big thing with my New York-based editors. For every
story featured, there were dozens behind them deserving of similar
coverage, but the opportunities rarely rolled around. To most,
it just wasn't clear how to approach editors and there
was little confidence that the editors wanted to hear
from them. Yet opportunities for online exposure were
ever expanding - and the need to be prepared for them,
never greater. Year after year I saw this repeat like a film reel
on a continuous loop until, one day, I recognized that
I might know the answer.

At that moment my glimpse became connected to my own
next step. What would the tool look like to help
people navigate their own PR and how would my
writing life funnel into the new publishing realities?

The day I took the first step toward designing a solution - which
has lead to DIY publicity workshops, my book, Recipe for Press,
speaking engagements, and a growing consultancy - was
the day I gave proper deference to my imagination.

Imagination nudged aside worry, insisting there was a
way to conjure interest, support, and a book (and while
I was at it, a completely unrelated and audacious enterprise
on the side making fashion accessories in paper).

Security was another issue. A wholesale change in career
with minimal investment on anyone's part but my family's
required an uncomfortable amount of risk taking. Very
quickly I was reacquainted with a vulnerability that comes from
exposing your most sincere efforts with the possibility of failure.
And yet a deeper sense of certainty and calm settled in, one that
came from connecting my vision to those I had been working
with all along. That I had a great deal in common with those I
envisioned helping led me to know that the act of creating, in doing,
is ultimately the measure of anyone's success.

BENDING
in the
WIND

the compassionate success of Kara Larson's
Tumbleweed

When the economy soured, Portland, Oregon shop
owner Kara Larson took caring measures to keep
morale high, customers happy, and employees in jobs.
The results: her best three years in business.

story by **Amy Flurry**
photography by **Sherri Diteman**

THE GREEN REED WHICH BENDS IN THE WIND IS STRONGER
THAN THE MIGHTY OAK WHICH BREAKS IN A STORM.
-Confucius

For many shop owners, the economic downswing delivered too strong of a blow to recover. Kara Larson, owner of Tumbleweed boutique in the Alberta Arts District in Portland, used the moment to distinguish her shop's values - an affection for quality over quantity - and to try something new.

For over a decade, Tumbleweed's core attraction was her own label's rotating collection of frocks in pretty prints and timeless, layerable styles. Along the way she also cultivated local emerging talents and incorporated other popular labels into the mix and even opened up a toyshop next door called Grasshopper. But everything was thrown off balance in 2009 when cost pressures began to plague small businesses. Vendors folded, in turn leaving shops like Tumbleweed, who had placed orders, short on stock. And even her customer's confidence was shaky, seeing so many small businesses in the community close their doors.

So with the same fabled feistiness that Kara opened her store (she opened Tumbleweed on a credit card and it took her only one month, driven totally on passion), she decided to make some radical changes so as to keep her doors open. Her first order of business: cutting her personal salary in order to give her employees raises.
"It just truly felt like the right thing to do at a time when everyone was in fear of losing their jobs," says Larson.

Another way Kara cleared the hurdle was to expand her house label to include basics like camisoles, t-shirts, and leggings. That decision required investing in machines to work in new knits, which kept her sewers in work and allowed better pricing and control of her stock.

The unexpected gift in her decisions was the elevated morale in her employees, a mood that extended to the store's shoppers. "I really believe that in seeing these adjustments positively affect our community, it changed what it meant for them to buy locally!" But it was a change in attitude toward other boutiques and kid's shops in Portland that reflects the biggest shift in how Kara does business today. "There's long existed an unspoken competition and comparison between shop owners," she says. "That kind of energy really zaps creativity and builds walls and maybe after so many years of doing this, I felt I had some leverage in making change. Somewhere along the way I just decided to let it go and concentrate, instead, on ideas that fostered friendships."

In one example of this new direction, she created a list of phone numbers of nearby toy stores that shared some of the same lines. "If we were out of stock on something a customer wanted, my staff could quickly call over to others and see if they were available so that we could recommend to our customer," she says. "We did the same for the few lines we carried at Tumbleweed that might overlap with other shops."

Initially, there was some skepticism on the other end of the line, but Kara says that, over the years, this extra step really caught on. "It really boils down to exceptional customer service, which is one area small businesses can better the big box experience. But it's also a small way of showing support for each other, of sticking together. We can share and all come out ahead."

tumbleweed
boutique

195

Something

to Treasure

A LUSCIOUS JEWELRY-BOX OF UNIQUE IDEAS
AND INSPIRATIONS TO CREATE A PERSONAL
TAPESTRY OF FASHION AND DECOR

· FEATURING MY CAMEO FABRICS ·

PHOTOGRAPHY BY DAVID BUTLER

Love it? Make it! PAGE Nº218 Nº224

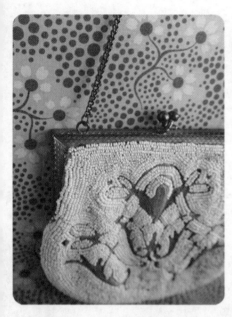

Love it? Make it! PAGE № 224

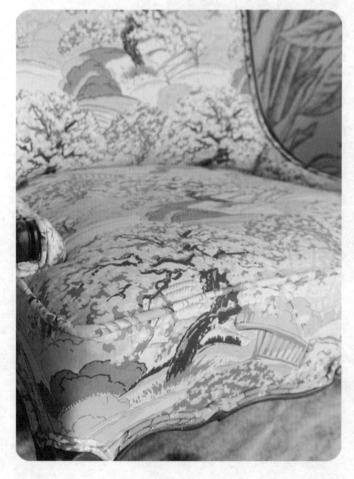

amy butler's Blossom Creative Suite

issue Nº 1

16 *projects!*

PDF DOWNLOAD ONLY $10

EASY • FUN • FASHIONABLE • FRESH • PROJECTS & PATTERNS

Something to Treasure

"No Sew" Fabric Tiles

Lined Vintage Trunk Lids

Pillows with Flanges

NATURAL HISTORY

Cameo Silhouettes

Quilted Wall Art

Lovely Layers Decoupage Vase

Custom Slipcovers for Square Poufs

Modern Painted Gourds

Grace

Graceful Lariat Necklace

Graceful Wristlet

Voile Flower Amulet

Voile Espadrille Laces

INDIAN SUMMER

"No Sew" Bolsters

Sheer Curtain with Fabric Panel

Sarong Skirt & Shawl

WONDER

Laminated Tabletop

It was very fun and exciting to make these projects for *Blossom*!
I've created so much fresh content that I developed this collection of
16 different projects from the pages of this first issue - The Blossom Creative
Suite is a pdf download of sewing, no-sew, painting, fashion, and home decor
projects with instructions and some templates. The 16 projects are shown at the
left, and they're all easy and fun with a great mix of skill levels for the beginning
crafter, as well as fresh ideas for the more advanced. Visit my website to download
this 35 page Creative Suite. I've kept the price low at only $10 for the 16 projects.
Enjoy! - xo Amy

VISIT
AMYBUTLERDESIGN.COM
TO SEE ALL OF MY
DOWNLOADABLE PATTERNS
AND CREATIVE SUITES!

Grace *Love it? Make it!*

Long Pom Pom Cowl
The Purl Bee

Free Tutorial at
www.purlbee.com/
long-pom-pom-cowl/

Japanese Sundress F1
From *Feminine Wardrobe*
By Kimiko Matsumoto

www.laurenceking.com/us/feminine-
wardrobe-twenty-one-beautiful-skirts-
dresses-and-tops-for-you-to-make

Japanese Ruffled Dress F2
From *Feminine Wardrobe*
By Kimiko Matsumoto

www.laurenceking.com/us/feminine-
wardrobe-twenty-one-beautiful-skirts-
dresses-and-tops-for-you-to-make

口ㅓ수 외ㅜㅓ *Love it? Make it!*

**Vintage Blouse
Ruffle Closure**
Inspired by
"Ruffle Fan Tutorial"
from Coletterie:

www.coletterie.com
/tutorials-tips-tricks/vintage-
details-ruffle-fan-tutorial

**Vintage
Bubble Skirt**
Inspired by "Very Easy
Skirt Refashion" tutorial
from Ruffles & Stuff:
www.rufflesandstuff.com
/2011/02/very
-easy-skirt-refashion.html

INDIAN SUMMER *Love it? Make it!*

Cinnamon Cami
Colette Patterns

www.colettepatterns.com
/shop/cinnamon

Sleeping Mask from *In Stitches*
Designed by Amy Butler

www.amybutlerdesign.com
/products/books_detail.php

Reversible Sunday Sling
Designed by Amy Butler

www.amybutlerdesign.com/buy

NATURAL HISTORY *Love it? Make it!*

Document Duvets from *In Stitches*
Designed by Amy Butler

www.amybutlerdesign.com
/products/books_detail.php

Clutch Handbag with fabric flower from *In Stitches*
Designed by Amy Butler

www.amybutlerdesign.com/
products/books_detail.php

Strapless Japanese Dress G2
From *Feminine Wardrobe*
By Kimiko Matsumoto

www.laurenceking.com/us/feminine-
wardrobe-twenty-one-beautiful-skirts-
dresses-and-tops-for-you-to-make

Miz Mozelle Dress
Jamie Christina Designs

jamiechristina.com/collections/
sewing-patterns-1/products/
miz-mozelle-dress-sewing-pattern

Clover
Colette Patterns

www.colettepatterns.com
/shop/clover

Shoulder Ties Japanese Dress D1
From *Feminine Wardrobe*
By Kimiko Matsumoto

www.laurenceking.com/us/feminine-
wardrobe-twenty-one-beautiful-skirts-
dresses-and-tops-for-you-to-make

Pretty Romance In Voile -
Boho Braided Necklace
Designed by Amy Butler

www.amybutlerdesign.com/buy

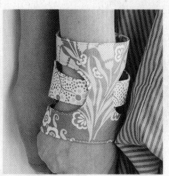

Alter Ego Cuff
Designed by Leigh Ann Tennant
as featured in Stitch Magazine

Download pattern at
www.interweavestore.com/Sewing/Patterns
/Alter-Ego-Cuff.html?SessionThemeID=22

The Charm Clutch
Designed by Amy Butler

www.amybutlerdesign.com/buy

Pretty Romance In Voile - Ruched Scarf
Designed by Amy Butler

www.amybutlerdesign.com/buy

Lisa Lam's "For Pleat's Sake" Bag
Designed by Lisa Lam

Free download at
u-handbag.typepad.com/
uhandblog/2010/08/free-bag-purse-
pattern-for-pleats-sake-tote.html

**Pretty Romance In Voile -
Peony Bloom Flower Pins**
Designed by Amy Butler

www.amybutlerdesign.com/buy

Barcelona Skirts
Designed by Amy Butler

www.amybutlerdesign.com/buy

Wanderer Ruck Sack
Designed by Amy Butler

www.amybutlerdesign.com/buy

The Gypsy Sling
Designed by Amy Butler

www.amybutlerdesign.com/buy

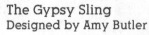

Reversible Sunday Sling
Designed by Amy Butler

www.amybutlerdesign.com/buy

Honey Bun Poufs
Designed by Amy Butler

www.amybutlerdesign.com/buy

Gumdrop Pillows
Designed by Amy Butler

www.amybutlerdesign.com/buy

Round Pillow
The Liberty Book of Home Sewing

www.chroniclebooks.com/titles
/the-liberty-book-of-home-sewing.html

Wingback Chair Upholstery "How To"
Designed by Amy Butler

Inspirational tutorials -
www.allthingsthrifty.com/2011/10/
upholstering-wing-back-chair-upholstery
.html

www.megeletto.wordpress.com/2011/02/20/
how-to-reupholster-a-wingback-chair/

Cameo Ornament Quilt
Designed by Amy Butler

Free Pattern
www.amybutlerdesign.com/products
/free_patterns.php

Book Covers
The Liberty Book of Home Sewing

www.chroniclebooks.com/titles
/the-liberty-book-of-home-sewing.html

INDIAN SUMMER *Love it? Make it!*

Sunny Quilt
Design by Purl Bee Blog

www.purlbee.squarespace.csunny-tied-quilt/

Quilt Size: 80 by 91 in [2 by 2.3 m]
Construction by Kerri Thomson
Instructions by Kerri Thomson and Sheila Brex

Fabrics shown are from my Alchemy Organic Collection:
Imperial Paisley/Blue Sky orab006, Memoir/Vapor orab011,
Sketchbook Roses/Cream orab009

This project is from the above blog, but with the alterations shown here!
You'll still need the blog info to get going on this beauty and jump in
with the free ideas below!

To show off my new Alchemy Organic Quilting Collection (44/45 in [1.1 m] wide organic cotton), I used only
3 fabrics instead of 11 (please see my construction notes). I did not tie off the quilt as it does in the pattern
but instead stitched-in-the-ditch* along the seam lines. I added a separate binding* to complete my look.
To make the quilt following my changes, here are the materials you will need.

MATERIALS
Quilt Top:
-1 1/2 yrds [1.4 m] fabric (Sketchbook Roses/Cream)
-2 yrds [1.8 m] fabric (Memoir/Vapor)
-2 3/8 yrds [2.2 m] fabric (Imperial Paisley/Blue Sky)
Backing:
-5 1/2 yrds [5 m] fabric (Sketchbook Roses/Cream)
Binding:
-3/4 yrd [67 cm] fabric (Memoir/Vapor)
-1 large spool of coordinating, all-purpose
sewing thread

TOOLS
- Scissors
- Rotary mat, cutter, and ruler
- Large safety pins
- Pins
- Tape measure or ruler
- Hand-sewing needle
- Walking foot for your machine
  (optional but a great foot to have for quilting)

Cutting:
- The Imperial Paisley print was treated as the "light" fabric in the pattern.
  Cut a range of nine 6 1/2 to 12 1/2 in [16.5 to 32 cm] strips.
- The Sketchbook Roses print was treated as the "medium" fabric in the pattern.
  Cut a range of nine 4 1/2 to 7 1/2 in [11 to 19 cm] strips.
- The Memoir print was treated as the "dark" fabric in the pattern.
  Cut a range of seventeen 2 1/2 to 4 1/2 in [6 to 11 cm] strips. I also added a 6 in [15 cm] and a
  5 3/8 in [13 cm] strip for a smoother progression of strips.
- For the binding cut nine strips 2 1/2 in [6 cm] by width of the fabric.

Construct the Quilt:
1. Construct the quilt top placing the fabric prints deliberately so the Memoir print is always between the
   Imperial Paisley and Sketchbook Roses prints.
2. To construct the backing cut the 5 1/2 yrds [5 m] of Sketchbook Roses into 2 pieces 2 3/4 yrds [2.5 m] in length.
3. Trim the selvage* edges, then sew the 2 pieces together along one long edge using a 1/2 in [1.2 cm] seam.
   Press* the seam allowance to one side.
4. Make the quilt sandwich as described in the pattern. Note: the width of the quilt top and backing will be
   very close.
5. Instead of marking and tying, I basted the quilt sandwich using safety pins spacing them every 8 in [20 cm]
   across the quilt.
6. Quilt the layers together by stitching in the ditch. Follow the Purl Bee instructions in the Mini Courthouse
   Steps Quilt for how to do this using your walking foot. purlbee.squarespace.com/courthouse-steps-mini-quilts/
7. Trim the quilt batting and backing to match the quilt top.
8. To finish the quilt, follow the instructions in the Courthouse Steps tutorial link above to make and sew the
   binding. Use a 1/2 in (1.2 cm) seam allowance instead of a 1/4 in (6 mm) for a wider binding.

*As you read through these instructions, any new terms may be marked with an * to indicate that you can find more
information on the fabric & sewing tips page of my website, (www.amybutlerdesign.com/products/tips). You will also
find fabric care information, a metric conversion chart, and other tips to help you with your projects.

INDIAN SUMMER *Love it? Make it!*

Colette "Nutmeg" Bralette & French Knickers
Pattern by Colette Patterns

www.colettepatterns.com/shop/nutmeg

Construction by Molly Frye

Fabric shown is from my Alchemy Organic Collection:
Sketchbook Roses/Cream orab009

This project is from the above pattern, but with the
alterations content shown here! You'll still need the pattern
to get going on this beauty and jump in with the free ideas below!

MATERIALS
I used 3/8 in [1 cm] fabric tubes in place of the ribbon for the bra. To make the bralette straps using fabric tubes you will need:
- 1/8 yrd [11 cm] of additional fabric.
- Tube Turner (we used Quick Turn by Dritz®)

1. To make the fabric tubes cut two strips of cotton 1 1/4 in [3.1 cm] wide by the width of the fabric.
2. Fold each strip RIGHT sides together matching long edges and sew using a 1/4 in [6 mm] seam down the long edge backstitching* at each end.
3. Use the Tube Turner to turn the fabric tube RIGHT side out and press*.
4. Continue to follow the pattern instructions using the fabric tubes in place of the ribbon.

Wide-Leg Lounge Pants (with updated instructions)
From Amy Butler's *In Stitches*

www.amybutlerdesign.com/
products/books_detail.php

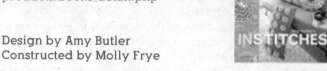

Design by Amy Butler
Constructed by Molly Frye

Fabric shown is from my Alchemy Organic Collection: Flora/Sapphire orab008

This project is from the above book, but with the alterations shown here! You'll still
need the book to get going on this beauty and jump in with the free ideas below!

For my Summer Solace story I wanted to update the Wide-Leg Lounge Pants from my *In Stitches* book. I made a few tweaks to the pattern: no trim along the bottom edge, widening the hem width for additional flair, and adding elastic to the waistband for a more secure fit. These changes are optional but if you decide to make them, here are the added Materials and Instructions you will need to follow:

MATERIALS
- 5/8 in [1.6 cm] wide elastic (the amount you will need is 1 in [2.5 cm] smaller than your waist measurement)

1. Follow Steps 1a-e of the instructions to make the Front and Back pattern pieces for the pants.
2. Use your yardstick to widen the hem width of each pant leg 5 in [12 cm] on the outside leg edges. Taper this width back up to the area around the knee.
3. Skip Steps 6c-d for attaching the trim.
4. Before inserting the drawstring in Step 7b, use the safety pin to insert one end of the elastic into one buttonhole, through the casing, and out the second buttonhole keeping the other end of the elastic on the outside of the first buttonhole.
5. Make sure the elastic has not twisted in the casing.
6. Have both elastic ends pulled out of the buttonhole openings. Overlap the elastic ends 1/2 in [1.2 cm], machine sew them together to secure, and then allow the elastic to go back into the casing.
7. Now you can insert the drawstring into the casing as instructed in the book.

INDIAN SUMMER *Love it? Make it!*

Wholecloth Tassel Quilt
Design by The Purl Bee and Amy Butler

www.purlbee.squarespace.windowpane-wholecloth-quilt/

Quilt Size: 76 by 86 in [1.9 by 2.2 m]
Construction by Kerri Thomson
Instructions by Kerri Thomson and Sheila Brex

Fabrics shown are from my Alchemy Organic Collection:
Floral/Coral orab008, Imperial Paisley/Ruby orab006

This project is from the above pattern, but with the alterations shown here! You'll still need the pattern info to get going on this beauty and jump in with the free ideas below!

I wanted to make the quilt as a full size instead of a baby quilt, and then add a fun tassel trim around the outside edge in place of a binding. I also did machine quilting instead of hand-stitching. Here are the additional materials and instructions you will need if you want to make these same changes.

MATERIALS   Note: Add extra fabric for centering and matching the fabric print designs.

- 5 yrds [4.6 m] 44 in [1.1 m] wide cotton quilting fabric for the Quilt Top (ours was from a local store, Chelsea House Designs)
- 5 yrds [4.6 m] 44 in [1.1 m] wide cotton quilting fabric for the Quilt Back
- 9 1/2 yrds [8.7 m] of tassel trim
- 1 pkg cotton batting (81 by 96 in [2 by 2.4 m]) (we used Cotton Classic® by Fairfield)
- 2 large spools of coordinating, all-purpose thread
- Hand-basting thread

- Chalk pencil or fabric marker
- Pins
- Scissors
- Hand-sewing needle
- Turning tool (such as a closed pair of scissors)
- Tape measure or ruler
- Walking foot for your sewing machine
- Darning or free motion sewing machine foot

TOOLS
- Quilting stencil - available at www.nancysnotions.com or your local quilting store

Construct the Quilt:
1. Cut the Top print into 2 pieces 2 1/2 yrds [2.3 m] long and remove the selvage* edges.
2. Sew the 2 pieces together along one long edge using a 1/2 in [1.2 cm] seam. Press* the seam allowance to one side.
3. Trim the Quilt Top to 77 in [1.9 m] by 87 in [2.2 m] long.
4. Place the RIGHT side of the Quilt Top facing up. Start at the center along one side edge and match the tape of the trim with the raw edge of the quilt. The tassels of the trim should be in towards the center of the quilt. Pin the trim in place, stopping at the first corner.
5. Sew a 3/8 in [1 cm] seam stopping 3/8 in [1 cm] from the first corner backstitching* at each end. Clip the threads and remove the quilt from your machine.
6. Turn the corner by folding the trim away from the corner forming a 90° angle with the trim you just sewed. Then fold it back even with the next raw edge and pin in place.
7. Begin sewing again at this edge of the quilt, backstitching as you begin. Continue to pin and sew along the edge, stopping 1/2 in [1.2 cm] from the next corner and backstitch again.
8. Repeat steps 6 and 7 to turn the remaining corners and sew the rest of the trim in place.
9. Cut the trim so it overlaps the beginning edge by 1/2 in [1.2 cm]. Backstitch again. Go back to each corner and clip away any of the trim's tassels that may be caught in the sewing.
10. Follow steps 1 to 3 to complete the Quilt Back with the second print.
11. Open up your batting. Lay it on a large flat surface and smooth out any wrinkles.
12. Place the Quilt Top on the batting RIGHT side facing up. Smooth out the fabric.
13. Then place the Quilt Back and the Quilt Top RIGHT sides together, smoothing out the panels and tucking the decorative trim in between. Pin the layers together around all of the edges.
14. Stitch a 1/2 in [1.2 cm] seam around the pinned edges leaving a 20 in [50 cm] opening centered along one side and backstitch at each end.
15. Cut the batting even with the Quilt Top. Trim all four corners in the seam allowance making sure not to clip your stitching.
16. Turn your quilt RIGHT side out through the opening. Use a turning tool* to gently push out the corners and pull out the trim. Press the quilt flat.
17. Fold the sides of the opening 1/2 in [1.2 cm] under. Next pin and slipstitch* the edges together using your hand-sewing needle and thread.
18. Attach your walking foot to your machine and slowly edge-stitch* around the quilt 1/4 in [6 mm] in from the edge.
19. Hand-baste* through all layers of the quilt following the tutorial.
20. Use your quilting stencil and fabric-marking pen to trace onto the Quilt Top the desired pattern you wish to stitch.
21. Now set your machine up for free motion machine quilting. Starting at the center of the quilt and working out to the edges, backstitch and begin to machine quilt following the guidelines you marked with your quilting stencil. Make sure to check the Quilt Back periodically to see that it is not shifting. Backstitch when you are finished machine quilting. Remove your hand basting when you are finished and press.

WONDER
Love it? Make it!

Spice Market Tote (with laminated tips)
an Amy Butler Sewing pattern

www.amybutlerdesign.com/buy

Design by Amy Butler
Construction by Kerri Thomson

Fabrics shown are from my Cameo Laminate and my Cameo Quilting
Collections: Tea Rose/Silver ocab019, Pressed Flowers/Carmine pwab096

This project is from the above pattern, but with the alterations shown here!
You'll still need the pattern to get going on this beauty and jump in with
the free ideas below!

I decided to make my Spice Market Tote out of my new Cameo Laminate. Because the laminate cannot be ironed directly, I substituted one layer of canvas for the fusible Pellon® Shape Flex® interfacing. More tips for working with laminates can be found on my website at this link: www.amybutlerdesign.com/pdfs/Laminated_Tips.pdf. Here are the changes we made to the Spice Market Tote for the laminate.

MATERIALS
- Cotton Duck Cloth Canvas 60 in [1.5 m] wide (1 1/2 yrds [1.4 m] for the small size and 1 7/8 yrds [1.7 m] for the large)
  in place of the fusible interfacing. We bought ours from www.jamesthompson.com.
- Plastic or Teflon presser foot for your sewing machine for when you are sewing on the laminate.

1. Follow the pattern instructions for cutting out the laminate.
2. From the canvas cut 2 Main Panel pieces and 2 handles. Machine baste* these to the Main Panel and handle laminate pieces.
3. Continue with construction of the bag. Top stitch* the side seams to keep the seam allowances flat.
4. Edge-stitch* the entire length of the handles to help keep their shape.

Origami Bag Set (with laminated tips)
From Amy Butler's *Style Stitches*

www.amybutlerdesign.com/
products/books_detail.php

Design by Amy Butler
Construction by Margaret Moore

Fabric shown is from my Cameo Laminate Collection: Josephine's Bouquet/Ink oca018,
Harriet's Kitchen/Sugar ocab016, Hopscotch/Lake ocab017, Tea Rose/Silver ocab019

This project is from the above book, but with the alterations shown here! You'll still
need the book to get going on this beauty and jump in with the free ideas below!

I decided to make my Origami Bag Set using my Cameo Laminate. Because the laminate cannot be ironed directly, I substituted one layer of canvas for the fusible Pellon® Shape Flex® interfacing. Please see my tips for working with laminates on my website at this link: www.amybutlerdesign.com/pdfs/Laminated_Tips.pdf before starting. Here are the changes we made to the Origami Bag set made with laminated cotton.

MATERIALS
- Cotton Duck Cloth Canvas 60 in [1.5 m] wide (7/8 yrd [80 cm] for all 6 bags) in place of the fusible woven interfacing. We bought ours from www.jamesthompson.com.
- Plastic or Teflon presser foot for your sewing machine.
- Binder clips instead of straight pins

1. Follow the measure and mark instructions for cutting out the bags using the laminate. Follow the same measure and mark instructions for cutting out the canvas.
2. Skip Step 2 in the instructions and machine baste* the canvas pieces to the WRONG sides of the corresponding laminate pieces instead.
3. Continue with the construction of the Origami Bags.

229

Velma's Mini Flying Geese Quilt
Design by Purl Bee Blog

www.purlbee.com

Quilt Size: 30 by 30 in [76 by 76 cm]
Construction by Kerri Thomson & Velma Heymann

Fabric used is from my Cameo Voile Collection:
Josephine's Bouquet/Ink voab011

This project is from the above pattern, but with the alterations shown here!
You'll still need the pattern info to get going on this beauty and jump in
with the free ideas below!

You can create your Mini Flying Geese Quilt by following this tutorial on the Purl Bee site using 44 in [1.1 m] wide quilting cotton. Or you can follow my additional instructions for making the quilt using vintage silk ties. Note that the size of the quilt and the blocks are larger than what is on the website. I also backed my silk tie quilt with voile from my Cameo Voile Collection.

MATERIALS
Quilt Top: You will need enough vintage silk ties to make seventy-two 3 in [7.5 cm] by 5 1/4 in [12.6 cm] flying geese rectangles. Each rectangle is made up of 2 different ties so you will need enough ties to make up a variety of different looks for each block.

- 1 1/4 yrds [1.1 m] 54 in [1.4 m] wide cotton voile for the quilt backing and binding
- 1 pkg of craft size cotton batting (I used Cotton Classic® by Fairfield)
- 1 1/2 yrds (1.4 m) of Pellon® So-Sheer™ interfacing (see Tip below)
- 1 large spool of coordinating, all-purpose thread

TOOLS
- Hand-sewing needle
- Scissors
- Rotary mat, rotary cutter, and ruler
- Pins
- Tape measure or ruler

Construct the Quilt:
1. Create your Flying Geese rectangles and Quilt Top.

    Tip: When working with silk ties, remember they are constructed on the bias* so the fabric will stretch and possibly fray. You can apply a light, iron-on knit interfacing*, such as Pellon® So-Sheer™, to the back of the fabric to stabilize it.

2. Follow the directions in the tutorial for layering the quilt, pinning, quilting, and trimming the backing and batting.

Optional Hanging Sleeve: Cut a strip of voile 7 in [17 cm] by the width of the quilt to make a hanging sleeve. Hem both short ends by folding 1/2 in [1.2 cm] to the WRONG side twice and edge stitching* 3/8 in [1 cm] from the fold. Then fold the strip in half lengthwise WRONG sides together, matching the raw edges, and press. Pin the strip to the top edge of the quilt back, matching the raw edges, and machine baste* to hold. Slipstitch* the fold of the sleeve to the quilt back.

3. Cut 3 strips of voile 2 1/2 in [6 cm] by the width of fabric for the binding*.

4. Make and attach the binding by following the instructions in the tutorial.

NATURAL HISTORY *Love it? Make it!*

Velma's Mini Flying Geese Pillow
Design by Purl Bee Blog

www.purlbee.com

Pillow Size: 24 by 17 in [60 by 43 cm]
Design by Amy Butler (inspired by Velma's Mini Geese Flying Quilt)
Construction by Kerri Thomson and Velma Heymann

Fabric used is from my Cameo Voile Collection:
Josephine's Bouquet/Ink voab011

This project is from the above pattern, but with the alterations shown here!
You'll still need the pattern info to get going on this beauty and jump in
with the free ideas below!

You can create your Mini Flying Geese blocks by following this tutorial on the Purl Bee site using 44 in [1.1 m] wide quilting cotton: www.purlbee.com/mini-quilt-flying-geese. Or you can use vintage silk ties as I have done here. Note that the size of the blocks for my pillow is larger than what is on the website. I backed my silk tie pillow with cotton voile from my Cameo Voile Collection.

MATERIALS
Pillow Top: You will need enough vintage silk ties to make thirty-five 3 in [7.5 cm] by 5 1/4 in [12.6 cm] flying geese rectangles. Each rectangle is made up of 2 different ties so you will need enough ties to make up a variety of different looks for each block.

- 3/4 yrd [68 cm] 54 in [1.4 m] wide cotton voile for the
  pillow back and binding
- 1 pkg of craft size batting (I used Cotton Classic by Fairfield®)
- 1 1/4 yrds [1.1 m] of Pellon® So-Sheer™ interfacing (see Tip below)
- Two 12 oz [340 g] bags Nature-Fil™ Blended Fiberfill
- 3/4 yrd [68 cm] 45 in [1.1 m] wide muslin
- 1 large spool of coordinating, all-purpose thread

TOOLS
- 1 pkg large safety pins for quilting
- Scissors
- Tape measure or ruler
- Pins
- Hand-sewing needle

Cutting:
1. From the voile. cut 2 strips 2 1/2 in [6 cm] by width of the fabric for the binding* and two 18 in [46 cm] squares for the pillow back.
2. From the muslin, cut 2 rectangles 25 by 18 in [63.5 by 46 cm] for the pillow form.

Construct the Pillow:
1. Create your 35 flying geese rectangles.
   Tip: When working with silk ties, remember they are constructed on the bias* so the fabric will stretch and possibly fray. You can apply a light, iron-on knit interfacing*, such as Pellon® So-Sheer™, to the back of the fabric to stabilize it.
2. Then sew these blocks into 5 columns of 7 geese using a 1/4 in [6 mm] seam allowance and backstitching* at each end. In each column arrange the geese so they are all facing the same way. Press* the seam allowances in one direction.
3. Sew the columns together along the long edges alternating the direction of the geese and backstitching at each end. Press the seam allowances in one direction.
4. On a smooth surface place the pillow top RIGHT side up on top of the batting and pin the layers together using the large safety pins.
5. Quilt as desired; I stitched-in-the-ditch* along the points of the triangles.
6. Trim the batting to match the Pillow Top.
7. Now take one 18 in [46 cm] square for the pillow back and along one edge turn in 1 in [2.5 cm] toward the WRONG side and press. Turn in another 1 in [2.5 cm], press again, and then edge stitch* in place. Repeat for the second 18 in [46 cm] pillow back square.
8. Place the pillow backs against the pillow top WRONG sides together, matching the outer edges and having the finished sides overlapping at the pillow's center; pin in place.
9. Make and attach binding to the pillow edges by following the directions for binding the mini quilt in the Purl Bee tutorial but using 1/2 in [1.2 cm] seam allowance.

Construct the Pillow Form:
1. Sew the muslin rectangles together with a 1/2 in [1.2 cm] seam allowance leaving a 9 in [23 cm] opening for turning.
2. Turn RIGHT side out, stuff the pillow, and slipstitch* the opening closed.
3. Insert the pillow form into the pillow cover.

231

Sash with Beaded Fringe (with updated instructions)
From Amy Butler's *In Stitches*

www.amybutlerdesign.com/
products/books_detail.php

Design by Amy Butler
Construction by Nichole Redinger
Finished Size: 5 by 90 in [12 cm by
2.3 m] long

Fabric shown is from my Cameo Quilting Collection: Hopscotch/Lake pwab095

This project is from the above book, but with the alterations shown here! You'll still need the book to get going on this beauty and jump in with the free ideas below!

I increased the length of my Sash with Beaded Fringe from my *In Stitches* book to give it a little extra flair! Here are the changes I made to the yardage amounts and the instructions for measuring and marking your fabric.

1. Fabrics: Purchase 2 3/4 yrds [2.4 m] of light- to mid-weight cotton fabric and 1/2 yrd [46 cm] of decorative beaded trim. I used vintage trim I had in my studio, but you can find similar trims at www.voguefabricsstore.com.

2. Replace Steps 2a-e in the instructions as follows:
a. Cut your fabric to make two 1 3/8 yrds [1.25 m] pieces. Then open up one of your pieces with the RIGHT side facing up. Fold it RIGHT sides together on the bias* of the fabric. Do this by matching one of the selvage edges* with one of the cut edges to make a triangle shape. Press the folded edge and then pin along the fold to keep the fabric from slipping. Repeat with the second piece of fabric.

b. On one folded piece of fabric, place the sash's left end pattern piece with the top edge on the fold* and pin it in place. Then on the second piece of fabric, place the sash's right end pattern piece with the top edge on the fold and pin it in place.

c. Now, starting on the folded edge of both fabric pieces and at the dotted line on both pattern pieces, use a yardstick and a chalk pencil and measure over 40 in [1 m] and make a mark on each fold. Then take your yardstick and place it at a right angle from the folds where you made your marks and draw a line straight out that measures 6 in [15 cm].

d. Using your yardstick, match up the end of this drawn line to the opposite end of the dashed line of the pattern piece on both fabrics. With your chalk pencil, mark a line down the side of the yardstick to connect both points. (You will have to move your yardstick to finish drawing your line.) Pin the fabric inside these guidelines you just made on both sash pieces. The marked area of each sash panel is 6 in [15 cm] wide by 40 in [1 m] long.

e. Cut the sash panels out along the ends of the pattern pieces and along the chalk guidelines you made in step 2d. Do not cut along the dotted lines or on the folded edges of the fabric.

3. Follow the instructions in the book for Step 2f.

4. Before starting Step 3, open up both sash panels, place the straight ends RIGHT sides together, and pin them in place. Sew a 1/2 in [1.2 cm] seam allowance and backstitch* at each end. Press the seam open. Then continue making your Sash with Beaded Fringe following the remaining instructions in the book.

Resources

I'd like to personally thank the advertisers from Issue #1 who originally appeared in the online version of *Blossom!* Be sure to check out their wonderful businesses!

Angela Walters - www.quiltingismytherapy.com
Bernina - www.bernina.com
Black Owls - www.blackowls.com
Celebrate Creativity - www.celebrate-creativity.com
Chandra - www.shopchandra.com
Colette Patterns - www.colettepatterns.com
Crafty Planet - www.shopcraftyplanet.com
Creative Bug - www.creativebug.com
Desperate Quilters - www.desperatequilters.com
DIY Show Off - www.diyshowoff.com
Enjoy Co. - www.enjoyco.net
Fat Quarter Shop - www.fatquartershop.com
Free Spirit Fabric - www.makeitcoats.com
Freshline Design - www.freshline.etsy.com
Granville School of Visual Arts - www.gsvaonline.org
Handel Group - www.handelgroup.com
Harmony Art - www.harmonyart.com
I AM Creative - www.iamcreativesolutions.com
Jamie Christina - www.jamiechristina.com
Jimmy Beans Wool - www.jimmybeanswool.com
Jo Totes - www.jototes.com
Judi Ketteler - www.judiketteler.com
Kalencom - www.kalencom.com
Kim Mettee Designs - www.colourstories.wordpress.com
Kollabora - www.kollabora.com
Making It Lovely - www.makingitlovely.com
Nancy Zieman - www.nancyzieman.com/blog
Parson Gray - www.parsongray.com
Purl Soho - www.purlsoho.com
Purse Patterns - www.pursepatterns.com
Quilt Home - www.quilthome.com
Refueled Magazine - www.refueledmagazine.com
Renaissance Ribbons - www.renaissanceribbons.com
Rowan Fabrics - www.makeitcoats.com
Rowan Yarns - www.knitrowan.com
Ruffles & Stuff - www.rufflesandstuff.com
Sarah Jane - www.sarahjanestudios.com
Skinit - www.skinit.com
Smart, Creative Women - www.smartcreativewomen.com
So Chick Handbags - www.shop.sochickhandbags.com
The Cotton Patch - www.cottonpatch.co.uk
The Fabric Shop Network, Local Quilt Shop Day - www.quiltshopday.com
The French Seam - www.thefrenchseam.com
The Makerie - www.themakerie.com
The Scarlet Thread Quilt Co. - www.scarletthreadquiltco.etsy.com
Thread - www.threadfabricstore.com
U-Handbag - www.u-handbag.com
Valori Wells - www.valoriwells.com
Where Women Cook - www.wherewomencook.com
Where Women Create - www.wherewomencreate.com
XLN - www.xln.com.au

Contributors

And another heartfelt thanks to our fantastic contributors...

Granville School of Visual Arts - Beautiful Minds - www.gsvaonline.org
I AM Creative - The Leap - www.iamcreativesolutions.com
Kim Mettee Designs - Colour Stories - www.colourstories.wordpress.com
Meg Nocero - Quotation Sparks - www.megnocero.com
Recipe for Press - The Right Mix - www.recipeforpress.com
Smart, Creative Women - Shine - www.smartcreativewomen.com
Sunny Meadow Farms - Taking Root - www.oursunnymeadows.com
Tumbleweed Boutique - Bending in the Wind - www.tumbleweedboutique.typepad.com

thank you
for spending your time with Blossom!

It's my sincere hope that you've found a little piece of inspiration to make your day shine!

{ create *love*

express *beauty*

be *kind* }

xo amy

amy butler's
Blossom
magazine

issue
№ 1

{ create *love*
express *beauty*
be *kind* }

ISSUE #2

Amy Butler's
BLOSSOM
Magazine

issue
Nº 2

create *love*
express *beauty*
be *kind*

WELCOME to

Blossom!

illustration by Brooke Albrecht
brookealbrechtstudio.blogspot.com

I AM so happy that you're here! You've landed in Issue #2 and it's full of inspiration that will help you tap into your creativity and your heart. I've included a delicious mix of how-to content, personal essays, and inspirational stories packed with links that will connect you to powerful life changing resources. What I love about *Blossom* is that it's all about seeing each other shine, and celebrating our collective journeys as we connect to who we really are. When we get to witness each other's joy, connection to bliss, wins, challenges, and real experiences we recognize that same passion inside of us. It makes us remember "yeah, this is possible, this is who I AM." I can have a life I love. I can trust in connecting with my purpose and have the courage to take the journey, and unearth my magnificence." The truth is we're already perfection, we're already complete, we're just in various stages of remembering. That's why it's so important we live a life we love. The inspiration and love that is created when we thrive from this place shifts the universe and reminds us all of our brilliance. When we shine, the world shines too, and when we're shining, we're happy and living from our heart.

We have countless opportunities to pay attention to our heart's calling for love. These opportunities come in all kinds of forms: in synchronistic meetings with folks we've just met, in working through daily challenges or relationships where we can choose love over fear, and also in our conscious choice to source love by looking for it and seeing it reflected around us. Deep down we are all seeking an exchange of love. The groovy thing with love is, the more we look for it, and act from it, the more it shows up in our lives.

"When love is pure you become the embodiment of love.
This love is offered to none, denied to none.
It just radiates from you, like light
from a bonfire or dreams from a dreamer.
It kindles the spark of love wherever it falls."
Deepak Chopra, Creating Affluence

All of these images are from our Instagram HEART project submitted by all of you!
Thanks to everyone who participated by sending me your artistic & found hearts!
instagram.com/amybutlerdesign

239

TIME HEALS
ALL WOUNDS

I've had some amazing experiences over the past year that have helped me to expand my love radar. My "heart experiences" started happening more and more as I had a series of intense interactions with someone I love very much. I realized that I was holding onto my fears and beliefs about her, and recycling habitual responses. I found myself trying to control what was happening, and I was suffering and afraid of losing love from her. I sorted through my fears, got clear about how I wanted to feel, and realized that this wasn't about me. I also realized it was ok for me to let go and accept that what was happening needed to happen for our ultimate benefit. When I started to let go I began to feel the love that I needed, it was a feeling of deep love and compassion for her and for me, without condition. I had a profound sense of self acceptance that was inclusive and welcomed all of me, including my darkest feelings. I had an opening and an understanding that without my acceptance of my darkness, I couldn't embrace or choose my light. I felt open and connected and I started receiving physical hearts of all kinds! I started finding hearts everywhere! It was like a magical affirmation of love and it made me feel totally supported. And . . . they keep coming!

I know we all receive these love notes from the universe and when we start noticing them we start connecting to all that is, especially to each other. I've been so inspired and moved by this that I created a sharing forum on Instagram where folks could share their Heart Experiences. The response has been incredible and it feels so good to share our light with each other! Thank you to everyone for sharing your stories and images. These pages are a study in love from you.

Holding space for love keeps our creative mojo flowing, our hearts open and connects us to our dreams! The more we focus on love the more it grows in our lives. Try keeping a Love journal where you can take note of all your heart moments. Keep it simple and take 5 minutes every night to jot down feelings of gratitude and where you've found love in your day. Here are some examples: you can note where you've given or received love, where you've stayed open and shared love and compassion, or where that love and compassion was given to you or where you've had an overwhelming feeling of love in nature, or in an exchange with someone you don't know - like connecting with a smile. Any expression of love will hit the spot! The main idea is to see love in your life and have fun! Thanks for being here and for being you!

create love
express beauty
be kind

With Big Hearts and Big Love!
XO
Amy

FOLLOW YOUR♥

be mine

CONTENTS

SPECIAL THANKS!

Blossom *is a collaborative art piece, and it takes many hearts and many hands to create this big and beautiful story. I'd like to give a huge thanks to these folks for sharing their time, talents, and gifts that make this magazine so special. It's an honor and delight to get to work with you!*

Dave Butler, Thank you sweets for being who you are!! I love our life together and how our creative story at home and in our studio keeps unfolding and expanding into the most beautiful places. Thank you for your time, care, amazing talents, and passion. Blossom has a feel and voice that is guided and crafted most incredibly by your gifts.

My Studio Mates: Susan Robson, Sheila Brex, Mallory Theiss, and Molly Lancaster for being the collective glue that guides and balances our studio life. Thank you for your heart and for the love and care you put into your projects and how you create and care with such ease and grace. Dave and I love and appreciate you so much!

My Friends and Family for your love and unconditional support! And for the inspiration that fuels my passions for life and for Blossom.

For All of our Very Special Contributors, Hildie Dunn, Patricia Moreno, Clare and Kate from Achillea Flowers, April Meeker, Maryam Montague, Amy Parrish, April Rhodes, Laurie Gerber, Kelly Rae Roberts, Xanthe Berkeley, Courtney McWalter, Ed Shuttleworth, Ali Dejohn, and Shannon Kinney-Duh. What a collective!! Thank you for sharing and shining so brightly!

Thank you sewing goddesses for your talent and energy and for bringing sewing inspirations to life! All of us in the studio love and appreciate all you do. Molly Frye, Sheila Brex, Kerri Thompson, Mary Dugan, Anna Smith, Beth Huddy, Colene Sayer, and Margaret Moore.

Brenna Williams, our gorgeous model for my Hapi story!

To local friends and businesses, Deven and the team from The Village Flower Basket, Barb Franks from Footloose, the Granville Farmers' Market. Cat Run Ranch flower farm, Wisp Yarns, and Green Velvet Mercantile.

Thank you to all of you for providing us with the best materials to craft, sew, & decorate with! Westminster Fibers, Coats, Pellon, Chronicle Books, Fairfield, Sew To Speak, Coats Thread, James Thompson Manufacturers, Prym Dritz, Ikea, West Elm, Springfield Antiques, Beadsbysandy.com

from the cocoon of creative desire . . .

Becoming the Butterfly

the beautifully imperfect process of finding your voice

By Visual Artist

Kelly Rae Roberts

artwork by Kelly Rae Roberts
Photography of Kelly by Viv McMaster

I wasn't always an artist.
In fact, it wasn't until about five years ago that I leapt from a long, practical, and sensible career as a social worker to the seemingly impractical career of a full-time artist.

The journey into full-time art has been the journey of a lifetime, complete with all sorts of fears, challenges, and surprises. But it's also been a journey rich in meaningful lessons, the kind of soul work that has been life changing.

The journey of the last few years has taught me that the process of painting and creating art is a giant playground in which to learn a ton of life's lessons around healing, courage, imperfections, change, and so much more. Simply put, what comes up for us on the canvas, or in any creative process - the challenges, the breakthroughs, the breakdowns, the triumphs - is a mirror for what comes up in our everyday lives. And when we're willing to truly allow and surrender to the process of letting our art out, even with the fears and vulnerabilities along the way, we inevitably let love in. Our lives expand, our hearts widen, our spirit soars.

I've captured the essence of a couple of these lessons below. May they speak to your soul, and perhaps inspire you to consider how the creative process is so much more than just putting some paint on a canvas or creating a new sewing pattern - that it's a much deeper journey, an excavation of who we are and who we want to become.

Seeing beauty in the ugly stages

Every great creative endeavor goes through an ugly phase. The colors are a mess. There isn't any cohesion. It's a big blob of visual angst. Often, I'll force myself to find something I love about a painting that is in its "ugly phase" - even if it's a 1"x1" patch of pretty blue paint in the corner. Once I find something I love, I'll repeat that element to other parts of my painting in really big ways until the painting isn't so ugly. Moving a painting through its ugly phase is hard, frustrating, daunting. But I've learned that sticking with the uncertainty and moving a painting through its ugly phase is usually its pivotal moment into something really special. Of course, it's a valuable lesson about life off the canvas. If we can transform an entire canvas by sticking with it through its "ugly" phases, what can we transform in our everyday lives? What is possible when we search for beauty, even if it's a tiny patch of light in an otherwise terrible day? What is possible when we embrace the not so beautiful layers of our stories and create beauty from hardship and struggle? What if we transform a crisis into an opportunity for growth and change? Working with a painting every single step of the way is a great teacher, a beautiful daring metaphor for our everyday lives.

Imperfections history a story love

Once we've moved through the ugly phase of any creative process, there are still many imperfections left behind. Some were "mistakes" that became happy accidents and others are marks that simply show the wounds and history of battle if you will. I love the idea of viewing these "mistakes" and imperfections like wrinkles on our faces. They show the evolution and history of our creative process, gorgeous marks that tell the unfolding of a beautiful story - just like the lines on our faces. There is a certain level of generosity, if we're willing to accept it, that life off the canvas can extend to us during our creative process. I love that!

Being fearless and trusting the journey:

Our creative growth and possibilities require us to be absolutely fearless, to push up against our edges and get comfortable with being uncomfortable. Many folks will tell you that their best creative moments were those when they took risks and did something incredibly bold. The same has been true for me. The more I unleash my joy, paint my heart out, take risks, splatter paint in new ways onto a canvas, jump out of my comfort zone, and stop treating my painting like it's precious is the minute I make bold choices and do things I didn't think I could do. The result? Not only a joyful and fun experience, but also a brave and intuitive painting. My best selling and most beloved images have ALWAYS been created from this place of freedom. Of course the same is true in life. Being brave is a practice in being uncomfortable - and trusting that whatever happens, we can continue to make more brave choices in the direction of progress and forward motion. What would our lives look like if we took more chances? If we trusted our own voices? If were willing to do something we didn't think we could do?

Embracing the chaos and letting go:

When I first started painting, it was quite hard for me to embrace the chaos of the messy creative process. It felt like uncomfortable, uncontained, wild energy. Now, I like to think of the creative process as a beautiful mess. You know how sometimes your life blows up and you don't even recognize it inside the debris that comes with change, transition, and growth? It's kind of like that, and I've found that embracing the mess and the chaos on the canvas is an excellent way to express the angst that sometimes exists in my life as an important way to heal, express, and LET GO.

Before entering the creative life, I was quite uptight, a "control freak" who didn't love a messy kitchen, un-made beds, that sort of thing. But once I started painting, embracing the mess on the canvas and learning to let go a bit, the dirty dishes in the sink and the piled up laundry didn't bother me as much. My threshold for living in an imperfectly perfect home began to expand as did my ability to live a perfectly imperfect life. So I want to invite you to be conscious of these shifts within yourself, too. Lean into the discomfort, the joys, the play, and begin to trust the process that not only unfolds in your creative process, but also in your life. It all matters.

Self compassion:

Allowing a creative project to emerge - whether it's a panting, or writing, or a design project - is sort of like parenting or nurturing a child. When we give our kids permission to be who they are and ALLOW them to emerge and grow and discover and take risks and make mistakes, when we encourage them to embrace the struggles, to work it out, to keep going, to be brave, when we loosen the reins just a bit. Then something happens. They bloom and blossom and grow wings and confidence and a better sense of self. They often surprise us and themselves through the process of becoming and transformation. It's a remarkable journey. The same is true with our creative projects and our creative spirits. They have a spirit all on their own. Our job is to simply show up, nurture them, and let the expression come through with as much permission as possible. Give yourself and your creativity all the same permissions you would give to your child during times of growth and transformation. Allow yourself to play, grow, discover, work through the struggles, and be brave. You just might be surprised at your own transformation of growth.

BLOOM

IN WEST HAMSTEAD

A TINY FLORIST SHOP
IN WEST LONDON
BURSTS
WITH CREATIVE ENERGY
AND SPIRITED STYLE.

ACHILLEA
FLORISTS

by Clare Emburey

photography by
Xanthe Berkeley
& Amy Butler

Our Story

Kate and myself opened Achillea in October 2010, after a chance meeting at our local Farmers' Market that same summer. We have known each other since I was about 5 years old as I grew up and went to school with her two daughters. I always found Kate's house so interesting when I went over to play, there were collections of beautiful trinkets from her travels and an enviable collection of old tins, as well as the most amazing conservatory filled with masses of house plants hanging and climbing and encroaching slightly on the living space! I would say that Kate's collecting definitely had an influence on me and I went away and started a few collections of my own!

By the time we were reunited that summer I had been working for a fantastic florist but felt it was time to move on. Kate had recently moved from the family home into a beautiful garden flat and fancied fulfilling a long term dream to work with flowers and open a shop. It was over a glass of wine and a few nibbles that our project began, and less than three months later we had a shop and were open to the public. It was all so serendipitous, I had been worried and nervous, but all these good things just kept on happening and I think we both felt it was all just meant to be.

Our shop is based in West Hampstead (Mill Lane), and ever since we opened our doors for the very first time, we have been really lucky to have some really lovely customers who have now become friends. We have done countless weddings for lots of loved up couples, worked on all sorts of events, and worked with some pretty big names in the Fashion, Art, and Flower World. I go to New Covent Garden Flower Market in Vauxhall about three times a week, and love buying the best of whatever is in season. Our style is quite relaxed, very much as if the flowers were gathered from a very beautiful english garden, and wherever possible we buy English flowers. Obviously at times this can be a bit tricky, but I think nothing can beat English grown sweet peas, garden roses, dahlias, bluebells, delphinium, scabious, cornflowers, and narcissus when they are in season.

Our shop can be found at 92 Mill Lane, London, NW6 1NL. We can be reached by telephone on +44 (0)20 7431 1727 and email at clare@Achilleaflowers.com. You can also check us out online at www.achilleaflowers.com, on twitter @achilleaflowers, facebook Achillea Flowers, and Instagram Achilleaflowers.

"Flowers are those
little colorful beacons
of the sun from
which we get
sunshine when dark,
somber skies
blanket our thoughts."
Dodinsky

"People from a planet
without flowers would
think we must be mad
with joy the whole
time to have such
things about us."
~Iris Murdoch,
A Fairly Honourable Defeat

SWEET PEA

"Every flower is a
soul blossoming in nature."
~ Gerard de Nerval

"To be overcome by the
fragrance of flowers
is a delectable form of defeat."
~Beverly Nichols

HAPI

IS A STATE OF MIND

by Amy Butler
Photography by Amy & David Butler

As I learn more about Synchronicity I can see it reflected in all areas of my life. Our trip to Egypt last December is a great example. The opportunity to travel there came together with such ease and alignment. We weren't looking for this trip, the trip found us. Now I can see why we were gifted with this adventure because it has had a profound effect on how Dave and I both experience our lives. We were embraced by Egypt in the loving connections with our friends with whom we traveled and by the people and places. It felt like a homecoming. For me I felt safe, at ease, relaxed, and completely inspired by everything; the ancient history, architecture, desert landscape, incredible textiles, decorative art, and especially by the people. The Egyptian way of life is open hearted, childlike, vibrant, and very much about living in the moment. There is a soulful grace and exuberance felt everywhere, very warm, very creative; flowing with an optimism grounded in ancient culture. I was moved by how such an old story of creation can inform in such a fresh and timeless way.

I find all travel incredibly inspiring and it stays with me informing my artwork and how I'm relating in the world. Sometimes my trips have a direct inspiration as is with Hapi. I was already starting work on my Fall fabric collection before leaving for Egypt and after returning home it was like I was given the last notes to a song. I completed my collection with my new Egyptian inspired voice and the result for me is a beautiful, fluid expression of what's in my heart. Hapi is the god of the Nile and is all about creation and moving forward. Hapi for me is an expression of the flow of creativity we all posses that moves from our heart and through our hands.

"There is a window between hearts, no more than that. Everything else exists within the heart." ~ Phillip Jacobs

I kept a daily journal of our experiences while we were
in Egypt and here are a few of the things I loved:

* Falling back to sleep after the call to prayer

* The sun in the morning warming our room as we
wake up to the sounds of birds outside our window

* Morning greetings with our friends sharing great
conversations about our experiences the day before,
eating bananas, cold crepes, and drinking instant coffee

* Relaxing boat rides on the Nile sipping tea, laughing,
napping, listening to music, and watching everyone smile

* Taking in the incredible color and natural beauty
and hearing it described through the eyes of my friends

* The Egyptian people and their sweet hearts, ease, and
welcoming spirit. We heard "Welcome to Egypt" from many people

* The pace of life in West Luxor, the simplicity and
joy in family, friends, and community

* Dancing with the village women

* Rock hunting in the Valley of the Snake

* Being in the presence of the historical sites - the temples
and tombs and all of their magic, and to understand it's all a
big beautiful story of creation. This creation is always expanding
and the ancient Egyptians knew how to express that energy.

* Our daily adventures and exploring, and
the smiles and hugs from my friends

* Knowing that the adventure never
ends and Magic is everywhere

Karnak Temple

284

EKTACHROME 100 Professional   EPN

the Nile Delta

Hapi FABRICS

amybutler   ROWAN

TRANSLATING THE SOUL
OF MY EGYPTIAN TRAVELS
INTO A PRINT COLLECTION
FOR ROWAN AND SEWING
PROJECTS TO INSPIRE
YOUR OWN HAPI
CREATIONS

M. MICHEL FOKINE, Chereographic Director of the Russian Ballet, and Mme VERA FOKINE, dancing "Scheherazade" Valentine

Love it? Make it! PAGE Nº 41b

298

Love it? Make it! PAGE Nº 416

Love it? Make it! № PAGE 416-417

303

Love it? Make it! PAGE № 41b

Love it? Make it! PAGE № 417

Love it? Make it! PAGE Nº 417

IMMERSED in MAGIC

take me where the magic never fades

Morocco Calling

that tugging on your soul is real

By Artist

April Meeker

Photography by
Maryam Montague
mymarrakesh.com

I have long held the belief that creative energy, left
unattended, metastasizes and eats at the heart like a cancer.
As humans, we are hard wired to create. We find great joy
in bringing something to life that didn't exist before. Each
creates in their own way. Some may be talented seamstresses.
Others are genius project directors. And still others find their
joy in teaching others to achieve their full potential. There is no
set way to be creative. The paths are wide and varied.

I went to Morocco to share my passion for living a creative life. I went to inspire
others who were searching. I went to be inspired in my own creative pursuits.

What I found in Morocco was magic. The Moroccan culture is steeped in mystical creatures
and folklore of all types. The architecture and design in Morocco bespeaks these beliefs.
Every color, pattern, and design has meaning. It is breathtaking to stand in a madrassa
(Koranic school) or palace and view all these elements working harmoniously.

I also found magic working in the hearts of those in our caravan. We came together as total
strangers, from very different walks of life. We came with our own hopes and fears. We hauled in
our emotional baggage and plopped it down next to our suitcases. We stood looking at each
other, wondering what would come next. We were vulnerable. We were unsure. We were excited.

How does one fully explain magic? By definition, it cannot be explained. I'm
unsure what exactly transpired in Morocco. I know that my heart broke wide
open to the people in our little group. It broke open to the Moroccan people
with their bright smiles and the simple, handmade life they live. It broke
open to the colors and landscapes. If hard-pressed, I couldn't explain to you exactly
how the events of my life brought me to Morocco. Maybe it was happenstance.
Maybe it was luck. I can only surmise that the powers that be conspired to
bring me there to fill my head with imagination and understanding.

Morocco has taken up residence in my heart. It has also found its way into my art studio
and wardrobe. A chunk of indigo sits coyly on my workbench. A pair of ruby red
babouche slippers await me at my bedside. I can feel the magic of Morocco pulling me
back, like a muse, beckoning me to come and sip from its fountain of inspiration.

Later this year I will answer that call. It is time to revisit my old friend.
It is time to share Morocco with others who are searching.

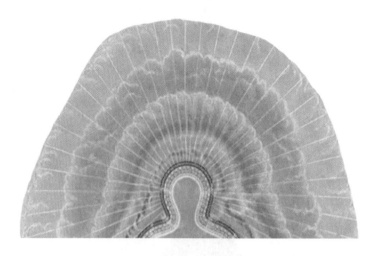

take comfort in knowing that it's all happening

For Your Benefit!

although it may not be obvious at first

Sage advice from SATI LIFE Founder

Patricia Moreno

When you ask, the Universe answers. But not always how you expect it to.

In one of my favorite books, The Seat of the Soul, Gary Zukav talks about authentic power and how when you set an intention and ask, the Universe answers with challenges or temptations so you can challenge your old way of being and choose a new way. Every time you challenge your anger, fear, or old negative habits and choose new, empowering ones you gain authentic power.

Have you ever decided you were going to stop eating sweets and soon get invited to a party or a function and sweets are all you see? That is a perfect example of the Universe giving you the opportunity to say no to the old habit and feel your power when you say YES to the new you.

If you decide that this year you want to be more patient, more proactive, more organized, or healthier, than you can bet the compassionate Universe will offer you opportunities to earn the new muscles you need to fulfill your intention.

Just like when you have the intention to walk from here to there, without your having to think about how to move each individual muscle, the intelligence of your body sets into motion the very complex process; when you set a clear intention to upgrade your life, the Universe will organize opportunities for you to have the new experience, but you will have to choose to take it.

Today, take some time to sit quietly and still your mind by simply focusing on your breath. Play some soothing music that helps you settle into your heart, then ask your heart what it wants. Listen, feel, and allow yourself to be guided by your higher self. Remember, once you know what you want and make an intention, the Universe will give you opportunities to choose this. Every time you want to react or do what you used to do, remember that the compassionate Universe is organizing opportunities on your behalf to be the change. It doesn't happen overnight but, remember, every step is a victory.

For today, let your mantra be
"This is happening for my benefit."

Learn more at SATILIFE.COM
and also find out about my newest course
"BEST YEAR EVER"

328

SOUL
in the
CLOUDS

the most compelling endeavor

Painting Through It

every creation is a personal expression

By Painter & Musician

Edwin Shuttleworth III

For years I have been living in the countryside of Granville, Ohio and commuting to work in the city of Columbus, forging a strong emotional connection to the land and the people who live and work in both places. In the fields, lines of trees, barns, houses, streets, garages, telephone poles and wires I experience overwhelming beauty, playfulness and humor, as well as aggression, sadness, and loneliness. It is this emotional response to the rural and urban landscape I see daily that I try to capture on canvas. I find inspiration from the most rural areas to the poorest parts of the inner city. To me the two share a lot in common and excite me as an artist, providing fertile ground for endless exploration.

There is so much that compels me as I pass the fields; patterns emerge from the partitioning with fences and trees, crop rows and vehicle tracks. The landscape itself may be unremarkable in terms of terrain, but the marks left by farmers working the land is what I find interesting not only from a compositional standpoint but as a visual record of their hard work and perseverance. The shapes of the trees and clouds have much in common in the summer - soft and billowing, moving in the wind. Trees in the winter may remind me of skeletons bracing against the wind. The sky is constantly changing, rarely if ever the same from day to day. As the rural transitions to the urban there are new and different features that strike my imagination; the lines created by telephone poles and wires spreading out in all directions; the fading paint on the houses, the patterns and planes of the rooftops, broken windows, cars, trucks, advertising, and street lights. There are no people in my paintings - I only allude to their presence in anthropomorphic ways, such as the putting faces in the houses and clouds, a solitary silo off in the distance. It is the unseen people I think of as I work and project their life experiences into the landscape itself, imagining who they are, what they are like, and how their lives have shaped, and been shaped, by their environment.

I arrive at my ideas through the use of photographs and sketches. I have taken thousands of photos over the years and sifting through them I find a few that look like they could provide good jumping-off points for a work. The resulting painting rarely if ever resembles the initial photograph because so much happens in my ensuing cage - match of a painting process - nearly as much paint gets removed in the process as stays on. The process is like a puzzle; the first stages being the easiest, getting trickier as I go on, until the very final stage where one false move can make or break the final result. For every "good" painting there are at least half-dozen or more that just don't pan out. Occasionally a painting will practically paint itself while many others hit a dead-end and are put aside for years before being revisited when I can see them in a new context.

Approaching Dreams — Oil on Canvas by Edwin Shuttleworth

Church of Sorrow – Oil on Canvas by Edwin Shuttleworth

Silverburst – Oil on Canvas by Edwin Shuttleworth

Western Sky — Oil on Canvas by Edwin Shuttleworth

The most instructive portion of my art education was growing up watching my father paint. Dr. Edwin C. Shuttleworth is now a member of the American Watercolor Society and has been painting for well over forty years. I spent many hours watching him work in his studio and he taught me more than any art school could have. I studied painting at Ohio State, as well as take courses at Columbus College of Art & Design and the Cleveland Institute of Art, but it was what I learned from my father that has had the most lasting benefit. He taught me to paint from the heart and spoke about reaching into one's innermost thoughts and feelings about a subject rather than simply "reporting" what you see. The importance of color relationships, values and compositions still need to be recognized, but merely interpreting the strictly visual aspect of a subject is not the goal. Rather it is conveying some emotion through it, such as the discomfort felt in the winter cold, startling sounds, threatening clouds and frightened houses. This can make a work really come alive with feeling and hopefully provide much more for the viewer to respond to.

There is a great book I have read titled "Art and Fear" which I highly recommend to anyone involved in any creative endeavor. The essence is that art is a process that one must learn to overcome through perseverance. When someone is convinced that their next attempt will end in failure they often just quit. The true artist is compelled to make art - it is not a conscious decision but rather the pain of not making art is greater than the pain of making it. Because it can be painful - it is difficult to have a great idea come to naught, face criticism and indifference. But when one does execute a truly good work and find people who enjoy it...to me there is no better feeling in the world.

Thanks for reading and I do hope you enjoy my paintings.
Please feel free to visit my website:
ecshuttleworth.wix.com/paintings
And/or drop me a line at ecshuttleworth@gmail
I'll be delighted to hear from you!

335

November `66 – Oil on Canvas by Edwin Shuttleworth

The Pink Door – Oil on Canvas by Edwin Shuttleworth

Pale Yellow House – Oil on Canvas by Edwin Shuttleworth

Cold Houses – Oil on Canvas by Edwin Shuttleworth

Elder Road – Oil on Canvas by Edwin Shuttleworth

Moonlit Path — Oil on Canvas by Edwin Shuttleworth

SMILE ON!

A SMILE IS THE SHORTEST DISTANCE BETWEEN TWO PEOPLE!

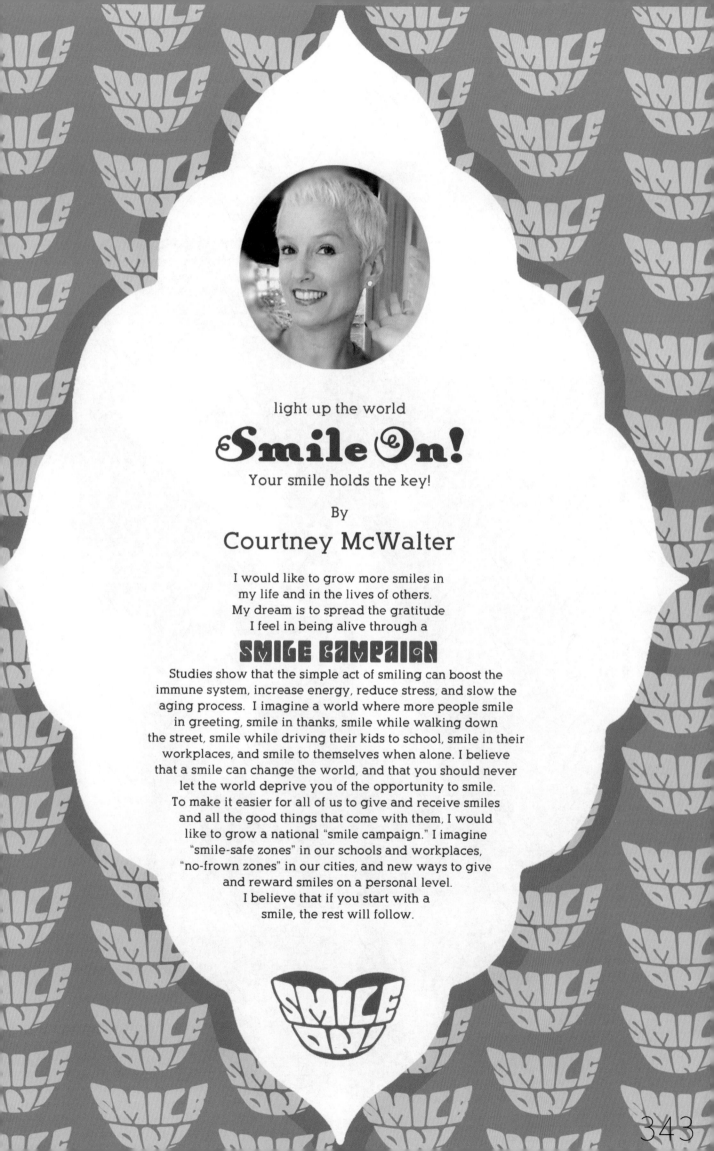

light up the world

Smile On!

Your smile holds the key!

By

Courtney McWalter

I would like to grow more smiles in
my life and in the lives of others.
My dream is to spread the gratitude
I feel in being alive through a

SMILE CAMPAIGN

Studies show that the simple act of smiling can boost the
immune system, increase energy, reduce stress, and slow the
aging process. I imagine a world where more people smile
in greeting, smile in thanks, smile while walking down
the street, smile while driving their kids to school, smile in their
workplaces, and smile to themselves when alone. I believe
that a smile can change the world, and that you should never
let the world deprive you of the opportunity to smile.
To make it easier for all of us to give and receive smiles
and all the good things that come with them, I would
like to grow a national "smile campaign." I imagine
"smile-safe zones" in our schools and workplaces,
"no-frown zones" in our cities, and new ways to give
and reward smiles on a personal level.
I believe that if you start with a
smile, the rest will follow.

The Power of
Pursuing Your Dreams

by Handel® Group Senior Life Coach
Hildie Dunn

As a life coach, I help people figure out their dreams
and what they really want. There are lots of types of
dreams and goals to achieve in your life. At the
Handel Group®, we break down a person's life into 18 areas:

*relationship to self, relationships with another, character
traits, family, career, time, body, spirituality,
money, bad habits, community, sex, romance, home,
personal space, learning, fun/adventure, health*

When I work with a client, we tackle every area of their life to
make sure they are dreaming and seeing the bigger picture of
what they can really have. It's about dreaming and being
happy and healthy in every area of your life. Here's how to start:

1) Grab a pen and paper and look at the list of 18 areas of life. Let yourself think deeply about
what you want in your life and choose three areas you want to address and create a dream.

2) For each area, choose one or two specific goals that you can accomplish in the next six months
that would make you happy and proud.

3) Once you have identified your dream, you are the one who can make it happen. For example,
if you chose home as one of the areas you would like to improve, make a plan to find a new place to
live that works better for you. If you are unable to move for financial or other reasons, redecorate your
home or get rid of the clutter. There are many things you can do to create a better home for yourself,
but if you don't dream, nothing will change.

Following your dreams is the act of loving life. Join me for "Dreaming in Color" - a weekend workshop
packed with ideas, creative insights, and inner exploration. Or try the Handel Group's flagship
workshop Design Your Life Weekend held in cities nationwide.

Love, Hildie

www.handelgroup.com

346

COLOR PLAY

*finding insight and
inspiration within
the colors of your soul*

By
Amy Butler

Photography by Amy Butler

I love playing with color! As an artist it's a very delicious ingredient in my daily life. I surround myself with color inspirations in my studio and I'm constantly cataloging my photos and images for the pure pleasure of interacting with the beautiful colors I've captured. The colors are downloading in my person and I pull from these inspirations all the time. Capturing my color experiences informs everything I do and expands my design eye and color instincts as I add more and more inspiration to my internal image bank.

In art school I learned to create color collages so I could easily share my color ideas for projects and presentations. This process of collage and color play has become an integral step in the creation of color palettes for my design work. Color collage for me is like breathing...it's meditative and connects me directly to my intuition and instincts, both of which we all possess. It just appears that artists are the keepers of this gift because we draw on our creative instincts on a regular basis. The truth is, everyone has an eye for color, we sometimes just don't know it yet. I've always believed everyone has a gift to bring the world and each of us is on our own unique journey to unearth this truth about ourselves. I started my "Create Your Unique Color Story" workshops last year with this idea in mind. The experience of color play perfectly mirrors our lives and exposes us to the degree of our knowingness or willingness to tap into and trust our intuition. This is also the place where we cultivate our intuition that shows us who we are and what our purpose is. You can only access your truth through your heart and intuition. Color collage connects you to this clear inner voice and opens the door for allowing what needs to come forward...to come forward. Like our lives, building a color collage is a step by step process of opening and allowing and trusting. The more we let go, the more easily it flows and the more fun we have!

I have loved watching my students reveal their gifts and seeing their faces light up when they've created their color collages and instantaneously know it's good, know it's true, and know it's them! Everyone leaves with a new door opened and a tool for practicing connecting to their intuition and heart. And, they have fabulous color palettes that they can use in their design work, home and craft projects. The experience alone is enough to cultivate your gift and the meditative activity of collaging, listening to your instincts, overflows into every aspect of your life, and it keeps *expanding*.

When my dear friend Hildie and I started brainstorming how we could combine our work together through Handel® life coaching, the ideas behind their Design Your Life™ Weekend events, and my dreams for bringing these tools to my creative community; a huge light-bulb went off and our Dreaming In Color Workshop was born! When you are working with color collage and nurturing your intuition you are in your heart and this is exactly the place where you can connect to and define your dreams for your life. It's here in this vulnerable, open place that you can learn to honor and tell the truth about what you really want while you dismantle the fears that are holding you back from your creativity and happiness. With Hildie's guidance and our collective love and support, we can share in a powerful life expanding experience. Just writing about this gives me goosebumps! Hildie and I are holding our very first workshop in my beautiful home town of Granville, Ohio. I hope you can make the journey and join us for this life changing event!

YOU are a gift! Big Love! XO Amy

354

Be beautiful Be yourself

357

modern designs
paper plunge

PARSON GRAY'S

SOUTHWEST
PASSAGE

TURN OFF THE MODERN WORLD TO FIND YOUR NATURAL VOICE.

photography by David & Amy Butler

*On a trip with Amy to the Grand Canyon, I found a new language
inspired by the astonishing, rugged landscapes. This is a place
that keeps a tight hold on its wonderous secrets and yet reveals more than
you can imagine - plant life growing in impossible crags and conditions,
vibrant and muted tones of earth color unveiled in cake layers,
not to mention the intuitive graphic nature used by Native Americans
to interpret their spiritual ties to these sacred sites. What I found aside
from amazing visual reference was a true connection to these energetic,
flowing wonders. I found my breath, and a quiet place inside my soul to
reflect on the importance of treating yourself as the land, and the land
as yourself. Because they are indeed, one.*

*This is a visual journal of how these impressions become the defining arch
for my newest designs, as well as reinforcing my way of being in the world.*

DAVID BUTLER AKA PARSON GRAY

374

TRANSLATION: PARSON GRAY PRINTS · 2014 COLLECTIONS EMPIRE & SHAMAN

"WALK OUT TO THE VERY EDGE OF YOUR COMFORT ZONE.
LOOK JUST BEYOND AND YOU'LL SEE A WORLD YOU
ALWAYS KNEW EXISTED, BUT IS ONLY NOW AVAILABLE
AS YOU OPEN YOUR EYES, YOUR MIND, AND YOUR SOUL."

The Earth is a living thing. Like our own bodies, it has areas
Arizona, is a vortex. A place of extreme health. An amplifier for
what you bring into it. Every person has a different opinion

Within the Sedona field, there are four main vortex energy sites
journal hopes to capture the extreme beauty of theseamazingly
you want to see, feel what you want to feel." So if you come

VOR

A VISUAL JOURNAL OF SEI

of extreme health, and areas of faltering energy. Sedona,
spiritual, mental, and even physical energy. It amplifies
and experience when visiting these mysterious fields.

Each unique, and each as beautiful as the last. This photo
uplifting sites. As with everything else in life "You'll see what
bring an open mind, some water, and your camera.

ONA'S ENERGY FIELDS

AMY & DAVID BUTLER

Cathedral Rock, view from the approach

Seven Sacred Pools in Boynton Canyon

Hearts Everywhere!

Junipers become more and more twisted
the further into the vortex hot spots.

387

Prickly Pear Cactus

Cairns at the Cathdral Rock vortex — Oak Creek

Bell Rock area

SYN
CHRO
DES
TINY

a photographer finds a new lens within

Seeing with Your Soul

how Synchrodestiny reveals itself

By Photographer

Amy Parrish

Photography by Amy Parrish

Have you ever felt guided by a force greater than yourself? Perhaps you see signs; making sense and creating patterns from the chaotic complexities of daily life. Or maybe there is an unexplainable pull in your heart, much like the waxing and waning of waves being lured by the moon. It's hard to deny that some coincidences can hold so much meaning and that even if they are purely random events, how we process those in our own mind can add immeasurable levity.

Last year I had the opportunity to visit Kolkata, India. I traveled with an American friend and met up with another from Mumbai, each of us volunteering for an organization, Blossomy (www.blossomy.org), that hosts a series of creative workshops each year for children and young adults who have survived or are vulnerable to human trafficking. What I discovered is that I became more transformed on that trip than probably anyone else we were wishing to inspire on our journey. This great awakening started at the Birla Mandir, a Hindu temple that draws in crowds of tourists and visitors each day.

I would love to share images from within this impressive marble structure, but as I approached the entrance, two security officers pointed to my large camera bag and informed me that I couldn't go inside. I had walked a few blocks from where I parted with a friend and we had left her car. By now it was near the end of a very long day and the idea of trekking back to the car alone in the dark to deposit my camera bag and then returning back once more on my own seemed overwhelming. I almost called it a night. "But," I finally told myself, "when will I have the opportunity to come back?"

Had I not been turned away at the doors and made the decision to return, despite my aching body telling me otherwise, I never would have found myself standing in the shoe-check room at that precise moment to hear someone calling to me through a cacophony of sound. In a city of nearly five million people, I'd been found by a newlywed couple whose wedding reception I visited less than two weeks prior. Neither myself or anyone I was with actually had known the couple when we attended the party, but had been invited by her brother who happened to be friends with the founder of Blossomy. And instead of the acknowledgement and momentary chit-chat that would take place in a typical American interaction, I was gifted with the most magical tour of the temple area. Not only did this couple act as enthusiastic guides, but they immediately felt like the type of dear friends you only see every few years. I felt warmth, familiarity, and a host of emotions. Every cell in my body radiated when we finally parted ways.

India became a different place to me that evening and, in retrospect, it was one of the most symbolic moments of my life thus far.

I stayed in touch with both the couple and the brother who had invited us to the reception. When I told the brother about my chance meeting at the Birla Mandir he sent me a web link to an in-depth definition along with his response: "Meeting with Shilpi was destined . . . we call it synchronicity."

"Synchrodestiny requires gaining access to a place deep within yourself, while at the same time awakening to the intricate dance of coincidences out in the physical world."
Deepak Chopra

The same week I returned home from India, a group of women began meeting at my house each Saturday for fourteen weeks to read through and discuss The Artist's Way: A Spiritual Path to Higher Creativity by Julia Cameron. A couple of chapters in I was rendered speechless when the author went into detail about the concept of "synchronicity," a term that I'd never been familiar with in all my life until my visit to Kolkata. During this fourteen week period, and for some time thereafter, series after series of coincidences collided in my daily life. At one point I tried to sketch out a spiderweb of connections; its strings so inextricably tied to one another and crossing over at so many points that I knew, without a doubt, that something greater than myself was leading me to specific people and places. I was being transformed.

Now I find myself growing more attuned to the world around me, opening up to the infinite possibilities it provides and allowing myself to welcome the unknown without being quite so fearful about what it may bring. In a sense, I'm actively learning to go with the flow and truly take the time and space to investigate my own heart when it feels, at times, that I'm paddling upstream. I also take time to pray and meditate and (as advised through one of those synchronous spiderweb moments alluded to above) remember to not just ask myself "What do you want?" but to also look upward (or inward) and ask "What do You want?"

This new level of awareness is still coming into being and, while synchronous events have likely occurred all my life, unseen in the peripheral, I've made the intention to pause, listen, feel, and be open to the endless connections and directions of life.

I could have never imagined...

And Yet, Here I Am.

First steps are the hardest, but before you know it . . .

By Sewing Pattern Designer

April Rhodes

Designs by April Rhodes   Photography by Suzanne Gipson

This is a love note, and a thank you note, of sorts, to express
my gratitude for a gift that has been given to me.

I could have never imagined, when I first began sewing, all the adventures my craft
would take me on. All the doors it would open. All the ideas it would inspire. My mother
was a sewer and her mother before her, as well as many of my aunts. It is one of the
few constants in my life. For as long as I can remember, I've always had love,
the support of my family, and the ability to make things (especially from fabric).
Sewing has forever been an outlet for me. A tool for self expression.

Throughout grade school I prided myself on buying clothes from the thrift-store and
altering them with my mom's (now vintage) Bernina. I loved having things to wear that no
one else had (even though some of those things were ridiculous)! My ability to sew gave
me choices. I had the power to take something and make it something else. It was liberating.
Then, about 6 years ago, after my mom and I opened our fabric shop, Sew To Speak, in
Columbus, Ohio, I really began to grow in my craft. I started using patterns and devouring
their lessons. However, I couldn't resist the urge to alter things a little. I don't know
when it happened, but I decided to try drafting my own patterns. I used large
sheets of craft paper taped together and even sheets of newspaper. I started making
my own designs from beginning to end. No more altering what already was or
using a pattern for a guide. I just did my own thing. And my own "thing" was
surprisingly wearable. It was thrilling!

I took up teaching sewing classes and soon found that I really loved guiding others
through the process of making. I could help them achieve something they felt good
about and we both came away feeling better about ourselves. I saw my calling. I taught
several classes a month. I taught hand-sewing and finishing, bags, accessories and
appliqué, as well as a simple draft your own skirt workshop. However, I never
taught any dress classes because the dresses I had sewn were "made up" and just
for me. Nevertheless, students asked for them. Then my mom started asking me
"when are you going to make that a pattern". . ."when do you launch your
pattern line, April?". . . all the time! I'm not sure how serious she was, but
she pushed me. I wanted to publish my patterns. I thought
about it often. It became a dream. Then a goal.

I wanted so badly to share my designs with others, but how? And would they really want them?
Who launches just one pattern? And my designs were so simple. Would they be too simple?
The constant affirmation from my mother and other close friends, saying that I needed to do it,
convinced me that it was NEEDED, is how I was able to trudge through all of my fears and
self doubts. All of my feelings about "not knowing how," or the possibility that no
one would really want my patterns in the end. No one knew who I was.

I walked through all the worries and published my first pattern in March 2013.
It was the first day of Spring and my first pattern, The Staple Dress. I was
shocked by how well it was received. More than shocked. It surpassed any and all
of my hopes. I was blown away. I felt so humbled, supported, inspired, and grateful.
Since the Staple Dress, I have released two other patterns, The Date Night Dress and The
Riding Peplum/Party Dress. The Staple Dress and the Date Night Dress are now available in
print and are stocked in shops all around the world, including ours!! My work is in places
I've never been! I don't have adequate words to express what that means to me! Self publishing
my patterns has been an absolute thrill. Helping women make fun garments, with clear and
simple steps. Building confidence and self-esteem through teaching . . . that is a dream come true!!
It is an unbelievable honor to be included in someone else's creative endeavors.
It feeds my soul and it's a connection that I never knew I always needed.
My heart is full.

AS IF
BY
DESIGN

THE
DATE
NIGHT
DRESS

THE RIDING PEPLUM / PARTY DRESS

THE STAPLE DRESS

APRIL-RHODES.COM

Throw out the rules
Believe in Yourself
be as a child in your creative world

By Artist/Blogger
Shannon Kinney-Duh

Photography by Shannon Kinney-Duh & Chris Duh

"I'm not creative. I'm not good enough."

That's what I used to tell myself.

And I started believing it, only deep down inside I knew in my heart, I was an artist and had gifts to share with the world. Yet, I let fear and self-doubt consume me for years.

My creative and healing journey began long before having children, but it wasn't until I started creating daily with my first son that I really stepped into the fullness of my own creativity. It was as if I finally allowed myself to let go of right and wrong. I stopped believing that there was a certain way to be an artist or a certain way to live life. I let go of the rules. I stopped comparing myself to others. I stopped letting fear paralyze me. Slowly, I started believing that I mattered, that I had a place in this world, and that I had gifts to share, too.

I started believing in myself and I learned how to make friends with my fear.

I saw my sons as toddlers naturally expressing themselves by getting messy and painting with their hands. They didn't hesitate or think about it first. They didn't agonize over it or plan it out or secretly tell themselves they weren't good enough.

Watching how my sons' intuition inspires them to be authentic without judgment is what allowed me to try creating for the pure love and joy of it, rather than striving to produce some amazing art piece. Isn't that so freeing? You mean, I can play with paint and I don't have to care what it looks like or even know what I'm making? Surely there is wisdom in that!

What I have learned from my sons' spontaneous creative play is that we are all born with this natural ability and the deep seated need to express it.

"Each of us must confront our own fears, must come face to face with them. How we handle our fears will determine where we go with the rest of our lives. To experience adventure or to be limited by the fear of it."
~ Judy Blume

Trust that you, your baby, & your body CAN do this.

"Wherever you go, go with all your heart."
~ Confucius

STRIVe FOR ImPERfecTion

The truth will set you free

Go deeper

bliss

find your cen

With inspiration and courage it's possible to return to that childhood essence, that all-knowing place that is creative, loving, and kind. It's our intuition - in our hearts - that embraces imperfection and jumps in with an eagerness for life with arms wide open. It's that gift inside that is there to guide us in life (if we find the courage to listen).

Watching my children create has reopened a creative door in my heart that self doubt and fear kept shut for many years.

It made me realize that my own negative thoughts and inhibiting behaviors were holding me back and keeping me small. I saw a direct connection with my thoughts and things happening in my own life. When I started changing my negative thoughts, "I'm not creative or good enough" to "I am a creative being and it is safe to be me," is when I started to see expansive change come my way.

I left a job I had been holding onto for years. I created my own business and created a simple work schedule around my kids. I started writing and making art and sharing it with others. I started to experience an abundance of joy. And I began connecting to other life-explorers from all over the world.

Awakening to the idea that what I focus on grows and that I am the creator of my life was the turning point in my creative healing journey.

We all get daily reminders on how to face and embrace fear, to surrender to what is, to learn to TRUST, and to open our hearts to the wonder life has to offer. Most recently for me, being a mother to three young children has been teaching me some of my greatest lessons so far.

My oldest son started kindergarten this past year. He's a very reserved kid and I was nervous about how he might react to school. It takes him a long time to feel comfortable in new situations. He is a listener and an observer. He takes everything in and assesses his surroundings before getting involved.

On the morning of his first day, I woke him up announcing, "It's your first day of school!" He smiled and was visibly excited. I started to go down the whole if-you-get-sad-and-miss-us-talk and he stopped me mid-sentence, "Mom, I'm not scared anymore." And that was that... He hopped out of the car that morning with a smile on his face and has since fallen in love with school.

His ability to walk through discomfort and face his fears has been such an inspiration in my life. I, too, just recently faced one of my fears when I gave birth naturally to our third baby boy. Watching my 5-year-old start school for the first time reminded me that staying open to the discomfort that comes when fear is present helps us grow - sometimes beyond our wildest dreams.

And, wow, did I grow.

Five months ago I experienced the most magical, amazing natural birth. I was completely present during labor. I remember occasionally reaching for my husband's hand. Just feeling his presence helped immensely. I kept my eyes closed and went inward. I felt so connected to this baby and I could feel him swimming into position with each contraction. In between contractions, still keeping my eyes closed . . . I was smiling.

Seriously, I felt bliss.

Although my two previous births were special in their own ways, I never got to experience a completely natural birth. Finally, that moment where I felt my baby traveling down with each push had arrived. Again the feeling of bliss came over me in the space between the pushing. The same phrase that my oldest son said to me on his first day of school had now become my mantra, I'm not scared anymore, played over and over again in my mind. It was an incredible experience. After 30 minutes of pushing, my baby was in my arms. Relief, happiness, and love poured over and through me, and poured over and through us all. From this most recent facing fear moment, my heart feels big and wide open. I'm not scared anymore. And, once again, I am changed forever. That doesn't mean that I don't still encounter fear. But the mantra that I learned from my son, I'm not scared anymore, reminds me that I can walk courageously through my fears. It's far too easy to let fear keep us stagnant and comfortable (like I used to do). We have two choices when we are up against our fear, look the other way and run, or use that fear as motivation to see what's on the other side.

The first day of school can be scary.
Having a new baby can be scary.
The journey of motherhood can be scary.
Trying something new can be scary.
Saying, "I am an artist and I am worthy," can be scary.
Change can be scary.
Being authentic can be scary.

But the truth is, change brings up fear and everything changes over time.
Our beliefs. Our bodies. Our kids. The challenges and
celebrations we experience. Everything. Life is impermanent.
Everything is temporary. To expand and truly love this journey of
life, you can learn how to celebrate change and celebrate fear.

Your life is a gift.
Listen to and follow the wisdom of your own heart.

Explore your passions.
Make mistakes.
Stumble and fumble along the way.
Let go of hesitation.
Go for your dreams.
Feel the gratitude.
Choose love.
Do what you love and love what you do.
Be yourself, always.
And embrace this adventure called life!

In addition to being a mom, my greatest passion is inspiring
others to awaken to the wisdom of their own hearts.

I created A Free Spirit Life as a place to celebrate the freedom
that comes from creating and living a life you love.

I write e-books and create e-courses like
"Inside Out: A Creative Adventure of Self-Discovery"
and "Mothering with heART."

I also do personal life-coaching sessions and write a blog
where I share my life's explorations and discoveries.

www.afreespiritlife.com

to find your inner artist, simply slow down and

Look at Your Hands

The personal journey to build a creative haven

By the Creator of the Makerie

Ali Dejohn

It's always hard to know where to start the story of how the Makerie came to be, but when I close my eyes and think about the very beginning, I can tell you it all began a long time ago, deep in my heart. Although I was too young to put it into words, creating and making things with my hands always fed my soul and took me to another place, where all was calm and peaceful and the worries melted away. I remember spending hours getting lost in drawing pictures that were filled with the tiniest details and finding so much happiness in such a simple activity. I never realized how powerful and healing my love for creativity was and what an essential role it played for my well being. How could I have known that at such a young age? But looking back, this was a most treasured gift. Children have the most incredible, natural innate wisdom and we have so much to learn from them!

Skipping a few steps ahead along the journey of life, I became a mom to my two little ones, my most precious dream come true. I always wanted to be a stay-at-home mom and after a wonderful career working for the Chicago Marathon, I was lucky enough to be able to do that. I already had such a love for creativity, but having children surely took my passion to new heights and I felt a fierce drive to foster the most creative family I could. My appetite for creative pursuits became insatiable! On an unconscious level, I think I knew what creativity can do for one's soul and wanted to plant as many seeds as possible in my children so they too, could grow up with creative loves of their own.

When I think about a turning point for me as a mom and how the whole idea of the Makerie came to be, I remember being in my mom's kitchen, the stay-at-home mom I had always wanted to be, and bursting into tears. As much as I loved being at home with my babies, I felt completely lost in who I was as a new mother and felt incredibly guilty for being in a place I had wanted so much, but still feeling like something was missing. It tore my heart apart even saying that out loud, but realizing why I felt lost was the first step in figuring out what to do and how important it was to find myself again so I was able to be the best mom, wife, daughter, sister, and friend I could be.

"Owning our stories and loving oursleves through the process is the bravest thing that we will ever do."
Brene Brown

As many can relate to, creative projects often fall to the bottom of the priority list. Just plain life feels full taking care of our loved ones, work, laundry, grocery shopping, cooking, errands (just to name a few) and it's hard to justify putting aside time to just make something. But as I began to make a little time here and there to slow down and use my hands, the person I knew slowly started to come back. I found myself feeling inspired, not just artistically, but in the way I set the table or how we discovered treasures on family hikes or even in the way I combined new ingredients together to make a delicious meal. In nurturing my own creative spirit, I was finding one of the best forms of self care and nurturing my family and friends because of it.

412

my own
two hands

MAKING
THE MAKERIE

"You can't use up creativity. The more you use, the more you have."
Maya Angelou

As I began to realize how powerful creativity was in my own life, I knew it was something I had to share with others. I felt compelled to create a space for people to escape the demands of everyday life, where they could make creativity a priority and be encouraged to just play. I wanted to show people that they were, in fact, creative in their own beautiful way and imagined a place where people could step off the conveyer belt of life, truly slow down, and take the time to use their hands alongside others that were in need of the same thing too. They could take incredible creative workshops led by outstanding, loving teachers, participate in morning yoga classes, eat healthy organic meals, and breathe the fresh mountain air right outside their back door. It turns out, these ideas that I imagined became the Makerie.

If anyone ever told me that one day I would have the chance to work with Amy Butler, I would have done a double take and wondered if they were talking to me. What a very special treat it was to get to know her when she taught at our Makerie Sewing retreat last year and witness first hand the amazing, heart-centered way she walks in the world. What I continue to learn over and over again is that when we share our creative selves, we have the chance to get to know someone in an intimate way we wound't have otherwise.

It was so interesting to visit Amy's color workshops last year to see how everyone's color palettes brought out a personality, without even spending time with them! I joked with Amy that if I was a student in her class, she would barely be able to see my palette, as my choices would all be so similar - a variety of very soft, neutral, light, and natural colors that all looked like one. I guess that proves my theory, as I'm most comfortable when blending into a crowd. What makes a weekend like the Makerie so special is that you can truly be yourself and it shines through your art, without even trying.

People often ask what it feels like to come to the Makerie and my answer is always the same. It's truly a different experience for each person and if they come with an open heart and let go of their expectations, it always ends up being exactly what they need. Hearing the stories and reading the extraordinary handwritten letters serve as a constant reminder of how important this work is and how healing, empowering, and inspiring a weekend like this can be. For each person that comes to the Makerie, I envision a beautiful drop of water falling into a pond, where the gentle ripples represent the love of creativity that is spread to each person's own little world. Amidst all the lives that have been changed by the Makerie, I can humbly say with certainty that mine has been one of them too. I am forever grateful for the personal growth I continue to gain along this journey and am honored to be part of such an outstanding creative community.

It's still hard to believe that what was once a wild little dream actually became a reality. I'm still not sure how I mustered up the courage to give this all a try, as I'm a person who is quite shy at heart and putting myself out into the world is not something that comes naturally to me. What I do know is that I felt a calling to inspire creativity in the world and there was a stirring in my heart that wouldn't let go until I listened. And so I did.

Being a mom remains the most precious, important job I'll ever have, and part of being the best mom I can be also means fulfilling a dream of my own at the same time. Wanting to be something in addition to a mom once filled me with guilt, but now inspires me to become an example to my children in hopes that one day, they will follow their dreams too. One of the most important lessons I've learned is that anything is possible if you follow your heart. There is always a way. Creating the Makerie is surely a dream come true for me and if I can, in any way, inspire someone else to go after their dreams too, then this is what the Makerie is all about.

"Don't ask what the world needs. Ask what makes you come alive, and go do it. Because what the world needs is people who have come alive."
Howard Thurman

Love it? Make it!

La Boheme Tote
Designed by Amy Butler
amybutlerdesign.com/buy

FREE Hapi Quilt
Designed by Amy Butler

FREE Hapi Window to the Soul Quilt
Designed by Amy Butler

amybutlerdesign.com/products/free_patterns.php

Honey Bun Poufs
Designed by Amy Butler
amybutlerdesign.com/buy

Gypsy Sling
Designed by Amy Butler
amybutlerdesign.com/buy

Book: *Nani Iro: Colorful Fabric Dress Book*
www.theworkroom.ca

Book: *Easy, Cute Straight Stitch Sewing*
by Yoshiko Tsukiori
www.bonanza.com

An Artful Piece Tote & Pillows
Designed by Amy Butler
amybutlerdesign.com/buy

Hapi Creative Suite
Designed by Amy Butler
amybutlerdesign.com/buy

Creative Ribbon Suite (featuring Hapi Ribbons)
Designed by Amy Butler
amybutlerdesign.com/buy

Resources

I'd like to personally thank the advertisers from Issue #2
who originally appeared in the online version of *Blossom!*
Be sure to check out their wonderful businesses!

A Free Spirit Life - www.afreespiritlife.com
Angela Walters - www.quiltingismytherapy.com
April Rhodes - www.april-rhodes.com
Bernina - www.bernina.com
Black Owls - www.blackowls.com
Blue Bird Chic - www.bluebirdchic.com
Celebrate Creativity - www.celebrate-creativity.com
Crafty Planet - www.shopcraftyplanet.com
Creative Bug - www.creativebug.com
Desperate Quilters - www.desperatequilters.com
DIY Show Off - www.diyshowoff.com
French General - www.frenchgeneral.com
Freshline Design - www.freshline.etsy.com
Handel Group - www.handelgroup.com
Handmaiden's Cottage - www.etsy.com/shop/handmaidenscottage
Harmony Art - www.harmonyart.com
Jimmy Beans Wool - www.jimmybeanswool.com
Judi Ketteler - www.juddiketteler.com
Kalencom - www.kalencom.com
Kelly Rae Roberts - www.kellyraeroberts.com
Kim Mettee Designs - www.kimmetteedesigns.com
Kollabora - www.kollabora.com
Lucky Lucille - www.luckylucille.com
Make It In Design - www.makeitindesign.com
Nancy Zieman - www.nancyzieman.com/blog
Parson Gray - www.parsongray.com
Purl Soho - www.purlsoho.com
Purse Patterns - www.pursepatterns.com
Quilt Home - www.quilthome.com
Refueled Magazine - www.refueledmagazine.com
Renaissance Ribbons - www.renaissanceribbons.com
Sarah Jane - www.sarahjanestudios.com
Skinit - www.skinit.com
So Chick Handbags - www.shop.sochickhandbags.com
The Cotton Patch - www.cottonpatch.co.uk
The French Seam - www.thefrenchseam.com
The Makerie - www.themakerie.com
The Scarlet Thread Quilt Co. - www.scarletthreadquiltco.etsy.com
Thread - www.threadfabricstore.com
Urban Baby Bonnets - www.urbanbabybonnets.com
Valori Wells - www.valoriwells.com
Where Women Create - www.wherewomencreate.com
Xanthe Berkeley Photography - www.xantheberkeley.com
XLN - www.xln.com.au

Contributors

And another heartfelt thanks to our fantastic contributors . . .

A Free Spirit Life - Believe in Yourself - www.afreespiritlife.com
Achillea Flowers - Full Bloom - www.achilleaflowers.com
April Rhodes - As if by Design - And Yet Here I Am - www.april-rhodes.com
Ed Shuttleworth - Soul in the Clouds - Painting Through It - www.ecshuttleworth.wix.com/paintings
Handel - Pursuing Your Dreams - www.handelgroup.com
Kelly Rae Roberts - Becoming the Butterfly - www.kellyraeroberts.com
Maryam Montague - Immersed in Magic - Morocco Calling - www.mmontague.com/my-marrakesh/
Sati Life - For Your Benefit! - www.satilife.com
Smile On by Courtney McWalter
Synchrodestiny - Seeing with Your Soul by Amy Parrish - www.amyparrish.com
The Makerie - Look at Your Hands - Making the Makerie - www.themakerie.com

Thank You
for joining me in my creative passion,
Blossom Magazine.
I'm so happy to be able to share it with you.
I hope you've found a bit of inspiration to
jump-start your own creative ideas!
xo Amy